A Special Loving

DOROTHY CARMADELLA

PUREWELL PUBLICATIONS

© Dorothy Carmadella 2006
A Special Loving

ISBN   978-0-9554158-0-7

Published by Purewell Publications
Flat 3
Purewell Court
Court Close
Christchurch
Dorset
BH23 3PG

A CIP catalogue record of this book
can be obtained from the British Library.

Designed & produced by:
The Better Book Company Ltd
Forum House
Stirling Road
Chichester
West Sussex
PO19 7DN

Printed in England

*This book is dedicated
to my mother.*

FOREWORD

This simple narration unfolds a love story which is not the usual human one of courtship and marriage but of a very special loving which some human beings are more endowed with than others.

This special kind of love is essential in a world shared by man and beast.

Man being the master, commands that the lesser be subservient and, unfortunately, there are some who would stoop low to conquer.

Members of the animal kingdom, having not the power of speech to fight for their rights, depend, therefore, upon that human being possessed with this extra-special sense of compassion to protect them and plead their cases when necessary.

The incidents related are based on fact and have left their indelible marks of happiness or sadness on my memory. If they are tinged with sentiment it is because every creature mentioned actually existed and like well-remembered and well-loved human friendships these, too, have a special significance for me.

ACKNOWLEDGEMENTS

I am grateful to my husband, Ernest Alfred Carmadella, (affectionately called "Eddie") for the patience he showed during the months that I was closeted in the kitchen, devoted to writing this book, leaving him alone in the sitting room, night after night and at the weekends; for putting up with slapdash meals and cold snacks; for his kindness in making me cups of tea and for carrying my typewriter each night from its storage place to the dining table upon which I worked after we had eaten.

I am indebted to my cousin, Elizabeth Paul, who helped to revive my memory in connection with many details concerning my voyages, by producing my original letters written to her at the time and which she had carefully preserved for the past twenty years.

I appreciate my brother Donald's kind criticism and would like to explain at this juncture that he was not keen that I relate the incident about the "cheeky mouse" fearing that readers, who do not know our family personally, would misunderstand and picture our home to have been infested with mice. This should not be assumed, however, as the "cheeky mouse" was the only one of its kind. A home containing cats could never effectively harbour mice and, moreover, kitchens in India are outhouses, set at a distance of thirty or fifty yards away from the main house with the servants' quarters usually adjoining them, hence the odd mouse that "may" have frolicked there.

I thank Mabel for her kind and generous help given at one of the most important stages of my work.

I extend my sincere thanks to many others who gave me encouragement when word got around that I was "writing a book".

Above all I express my very grateful thanks to my editor Mr J.C. Walls.

And, last but not least, I say "thank you" to my pussy cat who kept me company, playfully sprawled upon my typing paper on a side chair, thus creating the perfect atmosphere in which to recall a story such as mine is, whilst I toiled into the night.

CONTENTS

1

Part 1 ~ Family and Home

I am the third born in our family, my parents having had two sons previously. I have no doubt that they welcomed my arrival as I fulfilled their desire for a daughter. This, my father explained to me when I was older, was the reason for their having named me Dorothy, the name meaning "Gift of God", which they sincerely accepted me as being.

My father had a well-paid position in the offices of the gold mines in South India. He interested himself in sport and in the social club of the town and in numerous Church activities. He gave of his time and energy willingly, being generous and good-natured, but his death came prematurely, at the age of forty-one, after several heart attacks.

My mother was a disciplinarian. She was fastidious about order, cleanliness and neatness in the home. Consequently, we had a very organized upbringing in a well-kept home which always looked clean and fresh, with a place for everything and everything in its place. Virtuous and meticulous, she believed that children were to be seen and not heard and disciplined us by this rule. We were trained to be quiet, orderly, good and obedient. Her word was not to be questioned, trifled with or ignored and through this strict upbringing I learnt to admire, appreciate and fear her, though not necessarily in that order. Unquestionably, her teachings and training stood me in good stead in my later years.

Part 2 ~ Meeting God's Creatures

My mother's most redeeming feature is her compassion and love for animals. In handling an injured or abandoned

Mother (Ada) Father (Walter)
Donald (brother), Dorothy, Harry (brother)

animal, her loving skill excels all quality of love I have ever witnessed, and it is from her that I have inherited this same compassion for animals.

I recall, as a child, that the bedtime stories she related to me always revolved around anecdotes about animals and these tales were drawn from real incidents, which seemed to make them even more absorbing. She had a wealth of stories to tell and instilled in me the importance of showing kindness to God's creatures.

My introduction to them took place, not by word alone or through picture books, but from actual meetings with them within the walls of our home where pets abounded, not excepting the various furry and feathered visitors that happened along because of some plight that they had been rescued from.

Apart from the casualties she cared for, I clearly remember the mongoose that was encouraged to give up searching for food and shelter and to take up permanent residence in our hedgerow. I recall the cheeky mouse that was permitted to frolic in the kitchen after dark when Puss was well out of the way; my mother intentionally keeping her secure, whilst she and I carried small chunks of cheese to offer to the mouse. I remember how I tiptoed behind my mother, keeping very quiet, while she held out the cheese to the trusting mouse. It would nibble it out of her hand and then start round and make for its tiny hole in the corner. My mother, believing there were other little mouths down the hole waiting to be fed, would crumble more cheese and bread and cake near the entrance to the hole. Then, assured that she had done the humane thing, she would turn off the light, lead me out and shut the door behind us.

2

Pets and Casualties

One of our cats was a Persian, and a real beauty she was. She had long white fur and a sweeping brush of a tail, and was called Snow White. The other cat was a ginger striped tom and was appropriately called Ginger. In addition to these elegant felines we had two dogs. The male was short-haired with a ring tail. He had an attractive black and white coat and was named Tinker. The bitch was a smaller breed with a shaggy coat, and was known as Peggy. At the same time, we had a white rabbit and a small brown hare, the latter having been rescued by my mother from a neighbour's dog who had almost torn it to pieces. The poor creature was trembling and appeared to have a broken leg when she carried it indoors and placed it carefully on the floor for closer examination.

Great care and plenty of loving kindness was administered over the days that followed. Our little casualty was kept out of reach of the other pets, and day by day we noticed it grow stronger and bolder. It soon showed signs of recovery and, much to my mother's relief, the leg was not broken and the bruise sustained seemed to have healed.

At the end of a fortnight or so, the creature became restless for its freedom, so one afternoon my mother and I drove a distance out into the country. Once there, she chose a grassy hillside for the spot where our little friend was to be set free. Alighting from the car, cradling this small ball of fur, my mother walked a short distance up the slope and with a last farewell word and kiss she put the hare down. For a single moment he sat still, perched up on his hind legs, then looked up at us as though he were expressing his thanks, and in a flash darted away amid the tall grass! I saw my mother wipe away a tear as we started back to our parked car ...

On warm summer nights my parents and I would relax on our lawn. From above, a big bright moon shone down upon us and the sky flickered with a million stars. The world seemed so beautiful and quiet. The only noises that broke the stillness would be a croak from a nearby frog, soaking in the cool dampness of a flower bed and the crickets chirruping at the bottom of the garden. About us would be our pets. They were companions to each other and caused us great amusement with their antics. Snowflake, as the white rabbit was called, was quite at ease with the cats and dogs. He wandered about the garden freely all day in their company and was only secured in his hutch after nightfall. My mother never believed in imprisoning an animal or bird.

The antics would begin thus. Snow White would wriggle close to the ground, taking aim at Snowflake, who would in turn be crouching low, munching the grass. With a sudden leap forward she would make a clear jump over him and start the procedure again from a different angle. While she was thus performing, the dogs in like manner would be taking aim to surprise her! Tinker would bend his body, leaning on his front paws, wagging his tail lingeringly and growling gently in play. Sometimes Snow White would divert her aim and pounce upon him and then run off into the closest bush. All we could see then would be a pair of bright eyes shining through the foliage, until action commenced once more and she would jump out upon one of the dogs or chase a leaf in the gentle breeze.

This game would continue for lengths of time, each member thoroughly delighted by the fun and frolic. When they had had enough, Tinker would gently place a paw upon Snow White's head and she understood that the games were over.

My mother had an ingenious technique in introducing one animal to another, and I was always intrigued by the manner in which she conducted the ritual. By her side would be Snow

White and at her feet, with one brief command, she would have stationed the dogs. Snowflake, the rabbit, would be comfortably settled in her lap. She went through this routine every day and for lengths of time, talking in low, tender tones to the dogs, drumming into them, "Don't touch the rabbit" and "Don't chase Pussy", stroking Ginger and Snow White as the name "Pussy" was spoken. The reaction from the dogs astounded me. With their heads turned slightly askew, they would swear their allegiance by a ready wag of their tails and lick her hand fondly.

I cannot remember any aggression among our pets. In fact, at meal times, all four animals lined up beside each other for their food. In-between times, one of the dogs might poke a snout into the cat's saucer and more than often the cat would wander from its food to peer curiously into the dog's bowl and even sample something out of it. This behaviour was accepted without the slightest annoyance on the dog's part. Having eaten, the cats would perform their natural habit of washing their faces, bibs and paws meticulously, then they would settle down for a nap.

The pets had no particular places to sleep. Everywhere about the house was welcome to them, and quite often all four would curl up together into one large mass of assorted fur.

Cats always seek out the softest and most enviable places for their repose and Snow White had the habit of curling up on my father's pillow in the daytime. He never could tolerate this, but had long learnt that he would be fighting a lost battle had he uttered his dissent! At night Snow White crept into my mother's bed and curled up beside her, while Ginger invariably chose to sleep with me on the nights when he decided against prowling. Snow White was very much an indoor cat, only taking a walk in the garden when necessary. Ginger, on the other hand, loved to roam or sleep around in a shady spot in the garden. I remember my mother stringing a hammock between two shady branches for his benefit and into which he loved to retire in the daytime. He was a keen hunter and, much to our horror and disapproval, he brought back his kill regularly and laid it at my mother's feet. He would then be reprimanded, but there was no way to curb him except to watch him closely and quickly retrieve whatever he had chosen to catch.

I cannot now recall how we acquired our mynah, which, by the way, is an Indian bird allied to the starling. Mynahs are quite common in India and abound in trees by the roadsides and in the fields. They also nest in the gardens of private houses. Mynahs in captivity make excellent pets and are easily tutored to talk. Our mynah was named Jacob and he boasted a fine vocabulary. He was provided with a large cage which was suspended from a beam in the roof of our verandah. It swayed in an advantageous position where the sunshine caught it, but remained sheltered sufficiently if the weather turned wet.

As already indicated, my mother disliked caging a bird and accordingly the door of Jacob's cage was left wide open throughout the day to afford him the freedom of flying in and out at will. At night, after he had come in to roost, the door would be secured and the cage transferred into the spare room where Jacob spent the night in safety.

At the crack of dawn, my mother would bring him out in his cage to the appointed place on the verandah and, on opening the door, he would step out on to the doorstep of his cage, flap his wings wildly and fly across the length of our lawn into the mango trees at the far end of the garden. Perching upon a branch, he would jabber loudly, repeating some of the sentences and bits of nursery rhymes which my parents had taught him. Meanwhile, my mother would have cleaned out his cage and supplied him with a fresh bowl of water and seed. On completing this duty she would whistle or call him by name and he would fly back, perch on her shoulder and peck her neck gently. With him still positioned on her shoulder, she would enter my bedroom and allow him to transfer to the headrail of my brass bedstead. Inquisitively, he would flop down to my pillow and I would pretend to be asleep. Very gently he would peck me once or twice and break into his daily greetings which my parents had trained him to say. Ruffling his feathers and bobbing his head, he would summon, "Wake up, Dorothy" and "Kiss me, Dorothy". His chattering continued all day and delighted us.

Despite the freedom he enjoyed we had no fear of his flying afar or falling victim to a stray cat, because he kept to the limits of our garden. He was not afraid of our cats or dogs and even alighted upon their backs if any of them walked past his cage or whatever piece of furniture he had, at the moment, been temporarily perched upon. He never came to harm, though one day he did go missing. My mother released him in the usual way one morning and saw him fly straight into his favourite mango tree, but from then on her repeated calls and whistles, brought no response. Even so, she was not necessarily distressed, believing that he was preoccupied preening himself in the safety of the tree. But several hours passed and by then anxiety had mounted for his safety. We imagined the worst had befallen him and my mother and the gardener beat about the hedge and bushes in the garden in search of the remains of his body, but still no signs were found. Suddenly, just before lunch, a message arrived from a friend's house that Jacob was strutting about in their yard, loudly and repeatedly demanding, "Kiss me, Dorothy!" This identified him from among the ordinary mynahs that often alighted to join their poultry at feeding time, as I was the only child of that name in the vicinity.

On learning of his whereabouts, we immediately carried his cage there and in loving tones and with low whistles my mother attracted him into it. How pleased we were to have him safely back!

We had Jacob for many years, and as he aged he became resigned to his cage. He still enjoyed his bath in a large shallow receptacle we supplied him with, but because he could no longer roam the garden and peck about the lawn my mother and I would search the grass and collect juicy grasshoppers as a special treat for him.

Jacob's end came swiftly. He suddenly developed diarrhoea and within a few hours was dead. We never kept another bird.

In the earlier years of her life, there did not seem to be any likelihood of Snow White presenting us with a family and this saddened my mother a great deal. However, when she was well into her fifth year, she entered into a discreet courtship without our knowledge, and surprised us all by producing one tiny white kitten which was a replica of herself. My mother felt certain that Snow White was incapable of a second performance and therefore decided to keep Snowy, as the kitten came to be called.

A kitten, as any cat lover would agree, is a most lovable creature and nothing could be more heart-warming than to watch a mother cat teaching its kitten the ropes, so we got a great deal of fun in taking note of Snow White's careful upbringing of her offspring.

As Snowy grew, she acquired an independence as cats do. Unlike Snow White, however, who attached herself to the indoors, Snowy had a wanderlust and the minute she was able to she wandered afield and was forever getting lost. She used to disappear through little openings in the hedge and explore the gardens beyond our own. Once she was found meowing her little heart out, many houses away. On receiving the news of her whereabouts, we hastily retrieved her, but she never seemed to learn her lesson and on repeated occasions we had to rescue her from tall trees that, having climbed steadily, she was unable to descend.

A couple of doors away from our house there lived a family who kept an aviary. It was solidly built and was said to be cat-proof. However, Snowy decided to take a walk in that direction one day. It was late evening when we next saw her and a sorry sight she was. My mother heard her plaintive cries and rushed out to detect the trouble. There was our dear little Snowy, barely six months old at this time, lying prostrate across the bottom two steps of a flight of ten that led up to our front verandah. She was turning stiff and her body seemed arched. It was obvious that she had been poisoned and was in great agony. We rushed her indoors and summoned the vet, but even though he came in good time it was too late as Snowy had died. There was immense sorrow in our home over this dastardly action that someone had found satisfaction in executing, and we firmly believed that it was the family with the aviary who had resorted to this cruel deed.

Our garden was very large and partly forested with a thickly spreaded bougainvillea which rose to an unusual height. It afforded a sanctuary to a large selection of birds and there was a pair of grey squirrels living in a hollow halfway up one of the stouter branches. Wary of the dogs and cats, the squirrels kept their distance though my mother regularly distributed nuts in their path. One day, on returning from school, she told me that there was a surprise awaiting me if I would peep into the top drawer of the tallboy that occupied a corner in my bedroom. Eagerly I rushed to it and discovered, to my delight, a baby squirrel sound asleep on a bed of cotton wool. My mother explained that the baby must have dropped out of the nest, and whilst on the ground our cat Ginger had pounced upon it and brought it into the house. Luckily, it was not hurt but badly shocked. She could not easily return it to its hole, therefore we would keep it and look after it until it was old enough to be let loose in the garden.

Baby squirrel stayed for a precious four days only! My mother fed him on diluted milk through a glass ink-filler. He drank greedily at mealtimes and would then burrow into the cotton wool and soft rags which we had put into his nesting place in the drawer.

He was getting bigger and a little bolder and seemed to accept my mother's hand more readily than mine or my father's. But alas! His existence was short-lived. On the fourth afternoon when my mother went to feed him, no little nose peeped out. She dug gently into the folds of the rags and discovered, to her great sorrow, that the tiny creature had burrowed too deep into the nesting materials and had smothered itself. We could find no other explanation for his death. Only a couple of hours previously my mother had given him his usual drink and he had climbed happily on to her palm.

I had just returned from school to witness this sad turn of events, and we were very sorrowful, including my father when he came home from work later that evening. For several days after, we remembered our baby squirrel with regret.

One Sunday, a very unusual casualty came into our possession. It was a young hawk. I am justified in deeming it as unusual since these birds of prey seldom come to plight themselves, being noted for their speed and prowess. This young hawk landed in our backyard with a tremendous thud. My parents and I were grouped together at the time, and for a moment we thought it had come down for our chickens, but when there was no immediate movement they told me to stand back while they approached it slowly. It had a vicious glint in its eye and its sharp beak appeared ready to attack.

Having diagnosed its difficulties without actually touching the bird, my father assumed that its wing was injured. Plucking up courage and with its welfare at heart, my mother inched in and, regardless of the attack it might have made upon her hand, she extended an arm, at the same time offering caressing words as only she is capable of exchanging with furry and feathered visitors. Much to our astonishment, the bird allowed itself to be lifted up. She cradled it next to her body and carried it into our small spare shed where she placed it on some straw on the floor. She then offered it tiny pieces of raw meat which it ate greedily.

The next day, after it had accustomed itself to the new environment and to us, my father made a closer search at the wing which undoubtedly lay limp by the side of the bird, and he found it to be broken. Together my parents devised a means of supporting the wing in position with a couple of sturdy pieces of fine bamboo.

Apart from being immobile, the hawk ate its raw meat ration without fuss and even allowed my mother to put a teaspoonful of drinking water down its throat, by permitting her finger between its beak. It seemed very content on its straw bed and the regular feeds. We imagined that if the surgery which my father had attempted was not successful, it would have to remain our pet and my mother was already making inquiries about building it a decent-sized cage so that it should not be confined to the shed. However, about a fortnight later, on opening the shed door to take in its morning meal, my mother was nearly bowled over, for the creature, on getting the first glimpse of the outside, raised itself off the ground and crashed straight into her. What a shock she received! But a shout of joy came from her almost at once on realising that the wing must be on the mend. She held the door wide open, but our feathered friend could not get airborne again.

A few more days passed and then my father removed what was left of the dressings, for the bird in that first attempt to fly had undone quite a bit of the splint that was keeping its wing in position. As the rest of the dressing was removed, it got up on its legs and with a great force lifted off and flew past the door. It circled above our heads once or twice, then having done this successfully it gave a screech, pointed its head to the sky, shot up like a dart and was gone from sight.

3

Part 1 ~ Compassion

Just as kindness to animals and birds prevails, so, too, does cruelty exist and my mother made it a point to seek out and eliminate unnecessary suffering that is caused to dumb creatures.

There was a cruel practice among chicken vendors to tie their chickens' legs together and string them upon a bamboo pole which, thus bedecked with twenty to thirty chickens, rested horizontally across the back of the vendor's neck and shoulders. The chickens would travel in this manner, heads hanging downwards, for miles, as the vendor usually journeyed on foot from his village which might have been anything up to ten miles away from the town. He would set out in the early morning, arriving in our town close on midday. He would advertise his wares as he walked past our houses, and in the heat of a summer's day this was not a pleasant sight for the bird lover as the chickens would be parched and extremely weary from cackling their objections to being committed to such torture. The chicken vendor came regularly twice a week to our neighbourhood, and on the days that he was due my mother made it her business to watch out for him.

As he approached our house, she would beckon him into the backyard and beseech him to lay down the bamboo pole and unleash the tired legs, so tightly secured, and she would instruct our servant to bring two basins of water in order that the chickens could quench their thirst. In addition, she would throw handfuls of grain for them to feed on. After a restful half-hour or so, she would, very reluctantly, allow the vendor to go on his way, but she always permitted this with a heavy heart and sighed that if she were able to afford it she would gladly have made a complete purchase, not so much as to help the salesman but to rescue the unfortunate birds from their predicament. Sometimes she did purchase two or three, not because of the meat content they offered for the table but because they looked the most exhausted from the horrific manner in which they had suffered on their journey along the hot, dusty roads.

In the vicinity of our house lived seven or eight other families, and at least three of them kept ducks. We, too, always kept a half a dozen or so ducks in our poultry run. The houses in the district were built very much on the same lines, as they were provided by the gold-mining company for their employees, so there was much similarity in the set-up of the buildings. To mention just one characteristic of the plan, I remember that every backyard boasted a stone cistern with running water. It was about five foot square and a couple of feet deep. The uses to which each family put it were various, but the one in our house was certainly used to the ducks' advantage.

My mother arranged that every afternoon, between midday and two o'clock, this being the hottest part of the day, the cistern should be filled and our ducks led out to it for their enjoyment. The ducks naturally revelled in this luxurious pleasure, swimming happily around and quacking to their hearts' delight. It was always gratifying to observe the dry stone cistern transform within minutes to a noisy whirlpool of splashes.

Typically, and not content with showing consideration to our own ducks, it dawned on her that the ducks belonging to the other households along the way were not fortunate enough to be offered such happiness. Therefore, she struck on the idea of issuing invitations to the respective owners, arranging for them to send their brood of ducks to revel in our cistern. Accordingly, she drew up a roster as to whose ducks should come at what time and the owners were also asked to tie a different coloured tape on the legs of their ducks so that none should inadvertently become exchanged on the outing. The various families agreed to my mother's suggestion, and at the appointed hour our gardener was sent to collect the respective batch of ducks. What a quacking would set up as each happy brood waddled along the green verge, up or down hill as the case may be, through our back door and, heads down and bottoms up, dive into the cool of the water!

My mother supervised this ritual daily, ensuring that all got their full share of swimming, and retrieving small squares of fresh bread specially prepared in advance, which she threw to them as they swam happily around. I usually returned home from school in time to see the last batch of ducks indulging in their delights, and it was sheer ecstasy for me to watch their antics. The ground around the cistern would be swamping by then, for at least fifty pairs of webbed feet had waddled through the area in the course of the afternoon.

My father, fully occupied in his office far away from home, was unaware of these domestic goings-on. One could imagine his surprise, therefore, when one afternoon he returned home unexpectedly because of ill-health and retired to the bedroom for a rest. Suddenly he became aware of a loud pandemonium streaming through the window from the backyard. He knew that our own handful of ducks could never, in their wildest moments, produce such a magnified sound, so he made for the open window and was astounded at what he saw for he observed at least twenty ducks – some in the water, others preening their feathers on the soggy ground, encircling the cistern – and he gave a loud gasp of astonishment, believing that my mother had spent all the housekeeping money acquiring this great number of ducks. The possibility made him livid, but she soon explained the situation, and in his relief to know that he had not, after all, become the possessor of a farmyard of ducks, he laughed away his annoyance and accepted my mother's behaviour as he had long learnt that her entire life revolved upon doing good works for God's dumb creatures.

The sanitary department of our locality had the responsibility of capturing and destroying stray dogs that roamed the neighbourhood, but its ways and means of achieving this end were not necessarily humane, for the men, instructed to perform this duty, were no more than menials. Armed with strong wire and a stout club or heavy stick, they set out upon the roads to get hold of the unfortunate stray. We never actually witnessed how they took their victims captive, but when they had, the strong wire was looped tightly round its neck and the pitiful animal could be seen staggering reluctantly along to its place of slaughter. We never could find out the truth about how their deaths were inflicted, but hearsay informed us that the end was cruelly performed.

Sometimes, poison was administered which caused an agonising death, or, alternatively, the poor creatures were committed to a deep pit and from above, were stoned to death or clubbed at close quarters. It turned our stomachs over to learn of these horrifying details, and my mother, heavy-hearted from the realization of the agony and terror that accompanied such a death, did all in her power to save as many as possible of the strays that happened to be dragged past our house. She would waylay the man in his pursuit and plead with him to turn a blind eye to the stray that was scavenging the communal dustbins, erected at regular intervals along the street at the back of our houses. For a small bribe, he would sometimes agree to comply with her request and pass on as though he had not noticed the animal, or, if already in his custody, he would release it. Not every one of these animal pursuers was willing to abide by her requests, however, and because they were so poverty-stricken, they would bargain for a higher ransom!

On many occasions, my mother adopted the rescued animal, her first priority being to save it from a merciless death. Having accomplished this, she then had to devise a way of either finding a home for it or, failing in her attempt, convey it to the veterinary hospital and for a fee have it humanely destroyed. Taking this latter course of action meant that she was forever delving into the housekeeping funds, as the vet would not perform free of charge and there was no branch of an RSPCA equivalent.

Part 2 ~ Brownie

Among the many dogs that my mother saved from this situation there is one especially that I shall always remember. It was a small brown mongrel, and when she rescued him, he was infested with fleas and parts of his skinny body were quite raw with a skin infection. He was weak upon his legs and had a forlorn look in his large brown eyes. His condition reduced her to tears, but she was determined that if he had to die it would be on a soft bed of straw rather than at the harsh hands of the man from the municipal offices.

So she bribed the latter with a sum of money she could ill afford and took the dog over, and once in her possession she tended him carefully. First of all, she offered him some bread soaked in warm milk, which he gulped greedily, and this she followed up with small amounts of boiled meat. For a day or two she concentrated on building up the animal's strength, and when he began to show signs of improvement, she commenced treatment upon his sore skin. He was committed to the spare shed for the safety of the other household pets, and Tinker and Peggy sniffed about through the chinks in the closed door, impatient to meet the occupant, with one of two intentions in their minds. Either they were eager to make friends or impatient to see the stranger off! Their reaction was never proved, however, because Brownie, as we began to call our little mongrel, was kept permanently in the shed for fully two weeks while he grew in strength and convalesced from the mange. It was amazing to notice the change come slowly but surely. In less than three weeks we had a plump, healthy and happy pet on our hands. There was disagreement from my father who insisted that Brownie should not become an addition to the already large battalion of pets that padded our home, so my mother set about the difficult task of finding a suitable home for him.

Her efforts were soon concluded, however, when our gardener – a pleasant young man in his early thirties – asked if he could be allowed to own Brownie. At first my mother was diffident as she doubted whether a lowly peasant such as he could afford the expense of a pet, but he assured her that all comforts and proper food would be provided. Our gardener did not live on the premises, but came to work each day from a village about ten miles away. At five-thirty in the evening his day's work ended and happily he would set off on the long walk back.

On the day that Brownie was given into his charge, my mother worried about how the dog would undertake the long walk in the company of his new owner and discussed it with our gardener. Despite his sincere promise to carry Brownie part of the way, my mother did not readily believe him and begged my father to use the car, on this special occasion, to transport both gardener and dog. When the welfare of an animal was at stake it was evident that she would win the day, so my father had no alternative but to consent.

We all boarded the car and our gardener directed us on our way. Once we left the mining area, we found ourselves on a bumpy road leading along an avenue of shady trees. The drive was picturesque and a cool breeze blew through the open windows. The car left a cloud of thick dust as it sped along, for the road we travelled was no more than a cart track. As we approached journey's end, groups of village children cheered us and ran behind the car as it slowly rolled down the last few yards of beaten track. Finally, we came to a halt near a thick clump of bamboo. Our gardener explained that this was his father's land and pointed to some mud huts, with thatched roofs, on the borders of a freshly tilled field. One of these huts, he informed us, was his home. The car could not be taken any further because at this point all signs of a roadway ended abruptly, so we left it parked and, on his invitation, walked the short distance along a mud bank intersecting the field and soon reached the huts.

Within moments, word had got around about the shiny steel monster's arrival and we found ourselves surrounded by the villagers. Brownie romped excitedly in the new environment and immediately became friends with the curious villagers who appeared in numbers, grinning and exclaiming in the local dialect. We were dutifully presented to our gardener's old mother, wife and other family members, and one of them hurried away, returning with coconuts which he offered us as gifts. They welcomed Brownie fondly and one of the women explained to my mother that he would be well fed on oat cakes and goat's milk. My mother, however, had her own plans for supplying Brownie with meat bones and scraps from our kitchen, and each night from then on, when our gardener bade us good night, she personally handed over to him a curiously shaped newspaper packet.

Brownie was one of the many strays with a happy ending to his life, for he developed into a fine animal and grew enormously in size. He became so attached to his new master that he often followed him to our house, keeping a certain distance en route, lest he be discovered and ordered back. We were always happy to see him, however, and he would mingle with our pets amicably whilst he was there for the day.

4

Animal Love

At one time, my mother was taken ill and the symptoms she suffered were grave enough to warrant her admittance to hospital. Accordingly, she was taken into the neighbouring town and it looked as though she would be away for at least a fortnight. Her departure from home left me alone with my father and the household servants.

My mother's firm instructions on leaving, sick as she was, were that the pets should be watched carefully, and since the hospital was a great distance off my father could only visit her at the weekends.

The house was so lonely without her and I moped a lot. The animals, too, missed her, and for the first two days of her absence the dogs roamed the rooms and garden in search of her. At night, Tinker crouched under my mother's bed and whimpered most of the time. Peggy made no sound, but joined him under the bed, looking sadly at my father and me as though pleading for an explanation of my mother's long absence. Ginger soon seemed to forget, however, for within hours he returned happily to his favourite haunts in the garden. Snow White was the one most affected by my mother's leaving, and she went about from room to room, meowing loudly.

After several hours of plaintive crying, she jumped on my mother's bed and curled up at the foot. Her eyes looked wistfully around at every sound and she refused all food and drink. It was obvious that she was grieved and she pined in this way day after day. My father became anxious and tried all manner of ways to tempt her to eat. We stroked her and made a great fuss of her, but Snow White was not to be reconciled by our efforts to fill my mother's place. She had barely eaten a saucer of food for most of the week and my father feared she would fall ill and die before my mother recovered and came home. He had the added difficulty of reporting to my mother, either by letter or when he visited her, each pet's welfare, but he attempted to hide the truth about Snow White's fretting.

At the end of three weeks, my mother was fit enough to leave the hospital, but my joy of having her back again was not to be compared with the exuberant welcome that the pets gave her. The dogs leaped about her feet, barking joyously, and Snow White, on hearing her voice, came with measured tread from the bedroom. In soft, weak tones she mewed and rubbed herself against my mother's legs. She had certainly become very thin and my mother was quick to remark on it. However, within a few minutes of reunion we saw a marked change in Snow White's behaviour. She lapped up all the milk we offered and consumed a great deal of solid food as well. She washed and groomed herself with gusto, and a soft purr soon developed into a loud and continuous one as she settled comfortably in my mother's lap. For the first few days of Mother's return she shadowed her.

Ginger remained indifferent, however. He gave my mother no special welcome even when she embraced him. It would appear that he had not even realized she had been away for any length of time. He lived in a world of his own, dreaming in his hammock and entertaining himself fully with all that moved in the garden, be it a sprightly grasshopper or a crawling snail.

5

Farewell

One year we were invited by some relatives to spend the festive season with them. This meant a journey of about thirty miles by train and being away from home for at least three days, as we were to leave on Christmas Eve and start for home again the day after Boxing Day. We were all excited over the prospect of the trip. My brothers and I were especially looking forward to the fun we anticipated with our seven young cousins, who made up the family circle of the aunt's and uncle's home to which we were going.

Alas! A day or two before we were due to leave, our bitch, Peggy, was taken seriously ill, and her condition cast a gloom over the preparations for our holiday. My mother sat red-eyed and heavy-hearted beside Peggy's sick bed, for it appeared there was little hope of her recovering. She had an abdominal complaint and although the medicine which the vet prescribed gave a certain amount of relief, hour by hour we watched her frail life diminish until in the early hours of Christmas Eve she gave a last gasp and died in my mother's arms.

What a sad day it was! My mother was disinclined to board the train a few hours later, which was to take us on our way to the Christmas rejoicings at my aunt's house. She begged my father to put off the engagement, or to allow her, at least, to be excused, but he insisted on her coming with the rest of us.

That was one of the saddest Christmases my mother ever spent, and it seemed as though Peggy's death was the start to all the others that followed in close succession, for only three months later Tinker began to get ill, on and off. The vet remarked that his teeth were bad and this infection in the mouth was causing his stomach complaints. His breath gradually smelt more and more foul and he dribbled constantly. We were obliged to restrict him to a kennel and the outside shed, as it was not healthy for the other animals and even less so for us to have him at close quarters about the rooms. My mother swabbed his gums at various times of the day with a lotion prescribed by the vet. Even so, the condition did not improve and the final decision was taken by the vet who said it would be kinder to have Tinker humanely destroyed than to extract all his teeth and keep an animal thus handicapped for several years, without teeth. And so it was that Tinker, one beautiful sunny day, made his last journey in our car, with my mother, to the veterinary hospital.

Soon after Tinker was taken from us, Snow White, who was in her thirteenth year, gradually grew frailer and passed away peacefully in her sleep, so all we had left now was Ginger. He was getting on for eight years old, but was healthy and in good shape and he still maintained his independence, roaming the garden all night and dozing in his hammock during the day. He made regular appearances for his meals, but encouraged no further handling, ever eager to be about his business once he had eaten. Though three of our beloved pets had gone, the memory of them so haunted my mother that she was disinclined to fill their places for the time being.

At this very same period of time, my father's health was causing us deep concern. He had suffered one heart attack after another within a few months, and each attack kept him in hospital for a length of time. Towards the end of the year, he took to his bed, his condition deteriorating, and he finally passed away after having been an extremely sick man during the twelve preceding months.

The death of my father saw the complete break-up of our home. Indeed, for as long as I can remember my mother walked alone from that day onwards, and one must marvel at the independent spirit in which she conducted her affairs. To me she was the most unforgettable character it has been my privilege to know. She was the first inspiration who taught, directed and enforced into me a love for God, for how much nearer can one get to God than in the virtue that "Cleanliness is next to Godliness"?

Her second ideal lies in the close communication she has with God's dumb creatures. She places them in a favoured position, acclaiming her doctrine that man has the ability to prosper alone and drawing attention to man's ingratitude, no matter what one does for him.

In comparison, she upholds her belief that dumb creatures rely upon and exist only by the mercy of man's kindness, else they suffer and die from wanton cruelty and indifference. With this purpose in life she spends her days seeking out suffering creatures and, in a manner by which Francis of Assisi himself discovered Heaven, she pursues the work she believes that God destined for her.

Those who place animals in a position far removed from even the secondary level of man, would criticise bitterly and fail to understand such noble acts, but this special loving can be summed up in the verse of an English poet who wrote:

"So many faiths, so many creeds,

So many paths that twist and wind,

But just the art of being kind

Is all this sad world needs."

6

Part 1 ~ In Mother's Footsteps

Times change and as the years of turmoil that followed gradually sorted themselves out, I, too, had slowly grown from child to adult and launched out into a career that took me hundreds of miles from the old hometown. I experienced, for the first time, the fear of being on my own feet, coupled strangely with the joy of the freedom to be able to think and act for myself. I did my work conscientiously, gathered a vast number of friends about me and grasped at every opportunity of happiness that came my way. I resided, as most working girls away from home did, in the YWCA and treasure, to this day, a wealth of happy memories of the warm and lasting friendships under its roof.

In spite of my ever-increasing social activities, as contributor or participant, I still made time, driven by an inside force, to devote large slices of my day to the interests of animals. On the roads in India it is a common sight to encounter some form of cruelty or ill-treatment to animals. Stray dogs and cats abound everywhere, and in the intense heat of the Indian sun it is not a pretty sight to see a stray dog running frantically in search of a morsel to eat or stopping to quench its thirst from a dirty drain. Such was the fate of these poor animals, destined to survive only from the goodness of that passer-by who would willingly spare the time and thought to offer relief, however small.

I could not succumb to these distressing scenes which were part of my daily witnessing to and from my office. Therefore, I made it my duty to equip myself with a large thermos of cold water, a paper bag of buttered slices and a smaller thermos of milk. Also, in my cycle basket, I kept a saucer and a small enamel bowl. On happening upon a thirsty stray, or a scruffy cat, I would alight from my cycle, pour a little of the drink I carried into the appropriate receptacle, and cautiously approach the animal. Nine times out of ten, I discovered that its distrust of me would turn to assurance and it would respond satisfactorily by gulping down the refreshment offered. Somehow, I never saw the same dog twice though the cats inhabited the same area for long periods. Many a time I was delayed getting to my work because on the way I would have encountered some form of ruthlessness in which a horse or bullock was involved.

Love for an animal sometimes means making oneself look ridiculous in the eye of the spectator who is not on your wavelength. It may also mean facing up to insult and even injury to one's person when intercepting a cruelty.

In India, the animals are used largely in the fields, for means of transport, and also as beasts of burden. Animals are not a remote scene of the countryside, but actually brush shoulders with the hurrying crowds in the busy roads of cities and towns.

Part 2 ~ The Horse

One form of popular transport is the rickshaw which is a type of carriage drawn by a horse. The animal is literally worked to death since the rickshaw man endeavours to do as many journeys as he can, in order to earn a worthwhile day's takings. Therefore, he restricts his animal to no particular number of hours, starting its work at the crack of dawn and continuing with little rest until well into the night.

In the heat of the summer it was a common occurrence for a horse to drop dead in harness, from heat exhaustion and fatigue. Rickshaw men, it appeared, had a streak of adventure and a spirit more suited to a jockey, and often, when two or three rickshaws happened to be following each other's trail, this would evoke them into going completely berserk! Regardless of the occupants in the rickshaw or the safety of their animals, the respective drivers would obey a secret signal and immediately break into a wild race. They would wave their whips in a frenzied manner, scream commands and whip the horse into a gallop.

The roads were narrow and it was terrifying for the passenger, who held on tightly lest he be thrown off the shiny leather seat and into the road as the rickshaw is not completely enclosed. Apart from the anxiety of being ejected at speed, one had the additional fear of what might happen to the unfortunate animal if, whilst overtaking, an automobile chanced to appear and was unable to brake in time!

I witnessed many such accidents, and though my sympathy went out to the passengers involved it was the injured horse that drew my compassion. The medical aid always arrived within reasonable time for the human casualties, but the injured or dying animal was left unattended for hours on the roadside.

One sweltering afternoon I came upon just such a scene and long will I remember the appalling sight. The time was nearing three o'clock, and I was on my way to keep an appointment with a private pupil whom I tutored each day at this hour. I turned into the main road and was about five minutes' journey from my pupil's home when I saw a gathering of people. I dismounted from my cycle and made for the inquisitive crowd that had gathered at the brink of an empty ravine which occupied one side of the main road. There in its depth, some eight feet below, lay the crumpled mass of a horse. It was still alive, and I was informed that it had already been lying there for two hours. I was given to understand that two rickshaws were indulging in a race and at this juncture, where the road met a side turning, a car appeared unexpectedly, giving the horses a fright and causing the rickshaws to collide.

The other horse escaped injury, but this one sustained a broken back. The rickshaw man, having failed to get it upon its legs, to continue its journey, dragged it across the road and toppled it over into the ravine, thus abandoning his animal to die since it was no good to him any more.

Horrified by the details, I threw to the winds my responsibility to my pupil and quickly set about raising help. I sped on my cycle to the nearest private house and requested the use of a telephone. I had a speedy conversation with the vet, who was situated about six miles away, and pleaded with him to send help immediately, assuring him that I would pay for the expense of having the horse destroyed. I then returned to the accident spot to await his arrival.

But a full hour passed, and no signs of help appeared. I implored one of the natives in the crowd to fetch a bucket of water and to climb down to the animal and quench its thirst in such burning heat. I gave him a small fee for agreeing to do this and watched him with little satisfaction while the animal received this atom of relief from the pain and distress it was enduring. I made two further trips to that same private telephone and was told by the vet that help was coming.

It was near five o'clock by now, and I sweltered in the heat of the burning road without a tree to afford a bit of shade from the scorching sun. Then at about five-thirty a car, driven by an English lady, came into view. She broke speed, headed off the road on to the side and slowly came to a stop. I rushed towards her, and she asked if she could be of help. I quickly informed her of the situation, and told her of the long hours I had waited without any satisfaction from my repeated calls for help. She was horrified and wasted no more time. She told me that she lived only a few yards away and would be gone only for a few minutes. She intended to ring the police and the vet again and bring back her husband's revolver, so that if the authorities did not show up within a quarter of an hour of her telephoning, she was prepared to take the law into her own hands and put the suffering animal out of its misery.

True to her word, she returned, bringing a manservant with her, a bucket of oats mixed in water and the loaded revolver. She sent her servant down to the horse and he refreshed it whilst we marked time, scanning the road for help. Ten long minutes ticked away, then just as she was preparing to descend the ravine herself in order to shoot the horse, an animal ambulance arrived.

It would have been kinder and more practical to destroy the horse where it lay, but the attendants said this was not permissible and that the creature had to be taken aboard the ambulance, driven to the veterinary hospital stables and destroyed there. What torment was in store for that ill-fated horse!

There were, of course, two attendants and they urged two of the male spectators to give a hand. With much discomfort to the animal, they shoved and pulled it upon a wide plank, and this they directed back into the ambulance.

My lady friend did not stop at this point, for she invited me to give over my cycle to her servant who, she said, would take it safely back to her house and proposed I join her in the car. We were to follow closely behind the ambulance and see this heartbreaking event properly concluded.

On arriving at the hospital, the vet met us. He made a quick diagnosis and confirmed that the animal had broken its back and a foreleg. He then asked us to sign a paper, stating that we were holding ourselves responsible for the destruction of the horse and that all fees incurred would be honoured by us.

It was finally six-thirty when we heard the dull report of a gun from the stable yard, and knew then that our tormented horse was free from pain.

As we drove back there seemed so little to say. Sorrow robbed us of any inclination for conversation. This was our first meeting, and we had not even introduced ourselves properly, but the common bond of love for an animal in distress told us everything we wished to know about one another, and from that day Joan Danby and I became close friends. We found that we had a lot in common and fulfilled our spare hours motoring along the roads, endeavouring to help at least one animal a day.

I became a welcome visitor to the Danbys' home and enjoyed extreme kindness and hospitality. They had a Siamese cat called Ming and a mongrel dog by the name of Buster. I secretly wondered how it was that the cat was an aristocrat whilst the dog was an ordinary mongrel. One imagined that in the splendour of such a luxurious home both pets would have been pedigree. Apart from being a mongrel, Buster was bow-legged!

One day, several months after our friendship had been established, I plucked up sufficient courage to ask Joan how they came to keep a mongrel and was indeed touched by her story. She explained how, four years previously, on their first arrival in India, she found this puppy yelling in a ditch, with both front legs broken – the cruel deed of a villain. She rescued him, had his legs mended, christened him Buster and kept him as a companion for Ming whom they had brought out with them from the UK.

Buster and Ming were inseparable and he doted on the cat. No one in the house was allowed to touch Ming in his presence, which I had already learned, for on my very first visit to the Danbys' home, soon after the sad incident of the horse, whilst I awaited my hostess in the drawing room, Ming made a regal entrance, closely followed by Buster. Innocently I gushed over her, taking her up in my arms lovingly, upon which Buster flew at me, growling and holding me down by a firm grip on my hemline. I was terrified, and my scream brought my hostess hastily. I had, of course, on being arrested by Buster, flung Ming to the floor and trembled with thoughts of my being torn to shreds. Joan then explained to me how jealously Buster guarded Ming, and cautioned me about picking her up again whilst Buster was in the room. Apart from this jealous love he had for Ming, he was a very gentle and lovable dog, but Ming was his possession and he made it quite clear to all who attempted to disregard his feelings on this point. I also learnt that on both the occasions when the Danbys holidayed in the UK on their annual leave, they had taken Ming and Buster with them, by air, in preference to leaving them with the servants. Buster was indeed a lucky dog!

Part 3 ~ A Mongrel Pup

One of the very strict rules enforced upon the residents in the YWCA was the forbidding of pets. So, whenever I rescued a stray, I was obliged to turn to my friends in the hope of using their homes as a transient refuge until such time as I succeeded in finding a suitable owner for the stray kitten or dog that I was endeavouring to help.

Among the large circle of friends I had, there were six special ones whom I knew I could rely upon meeting my demands, for they were animal lovers themselves and therefore spoke my language. They also had the facilities of a spare shed or room in which to house a plighted creature. No matter what time of day or night I contacted them I could rest assured that a welcome would greet me. Scores of kittens must have passed through my hands via this scheme, and happily there was always a satisfactory end, though dogs were a little more difficult to place because, whilst most folk did not mind a cat, when it came to keeping a dog they invariably questioned its breed and were ready with a refusal when told it was a mongrel.

One hot afternoon I was cycling to an appointment at the other side of the town and my ride took me by the outskirts of a village. As I pedalled wearily along the dusty road, grateful for the patches of shade now and again and feeling the hot wind lash my face as it lifted up and around me, I suddenly became aware of yapping. I dismounted and listened eagerly. Locating the direction from which it came, I wheeled my cycle towards the wheat field in which I ascertained a puppy was in distress. Wading through the knee-high stalks for quite a distance, I suddenly caught sight of a young pup, barely two months old, secured tightly to a clump of tall stalks. I called out loudly, clapping my hands as well, to arouse attention should the owner be in the vicinity, but there was not a human being to be seen or heard.

The tiny creature looked worn out, but licked my hands gratefully when I undid the knots and picked him up. He might have been there for a couple of hours. His tongue hung out in the heat and the sweat dripped off it, but I quickly remedied that, for I had some milk in my flask which I gladly offered him.

There was nothing I could do but take him the rest of the way with me. I placed him in my cycle basket, and making tiny whimpering sounds he cuddled down and slept peacefully. I kept the sun off him by removing the shady hat I was wearing and placing it over the top of the basket.

On the ride back, I was in a dilemma, not knowing what I should do about him. I could not possibly take him into the YWCA. At that particular time, too, I was unable to approach any of my friends, as some of them were away on holiday and those who were left already had charge of a kitten or two I was trying to place. The only alternative was for me to take the puppy to the veterinary hospital, which was conveniently situated on the same road as the YWCA where I lived. The vet was known to me personally, and on some past occasions he had helped me to find homes for strays, so I decided that this was yet another occasion when I was obliged to seek his help. He was a very pleasant person by nature and showed a great deal of affection for the animals he tended.

He greeted me warmly and listened attentively to my request. The puppy, meanwhile, establishing in its little mind that I was its owner, cuddled faithfully into my lap as I sat talking to the vet. It seemed assured of its future in the comfort of my gently fondling it, but my heart lay heavy and I was almost in tears when the vet gave me no hopes. He tried to convince me that he had definitely had no requests for a dog and that the best thing possible was to have the pup put down.

The veterinary hospital closed at six o'clock, and it was now just five. Unwilling to accept his proposal, I was determined to try a little harder to save this small creature's life, so I begged him to keep it for me at the hospital for the time being, and promised that I would return before six with my verdict. He agreed but again underlined the importance of my arriving at a decision before six, since the animal could not be kept overnight even if I paid a fee for its stay.

I raced down the main road to a Chinese family I knew in the shopping area. They were wealthy art dealers and kept a magnificent home. I remembered that Mrs Chou, not so long ago, remarked that she would like a puppy, having lost their old pet a few weeks previously. I told her hurriedly the purport of my visit as the Chinese servant bowed me graciously into the elegant drawing room with its elaborate chandelier and expensive furnishings. I implored her to have the puppy but, fond of animals as she was, somehow this unfortunate creature was doomed, for she could not decide so quickly. She needed time to discuss the matter with Mr Chou who might not particularly want to settle for a mongrel. With time running out on me, I had no option but to take my leave of her and hurry back to the hospital.

It was ten minutes to six, and the vet was waiting for me. He had kept the puppy in his office and on its seeing me, by instinct and with gratitude for the brief kindness I had bestowed upon it, I was crushed with pity when it scampered up to me, greeted me with a happy little bark and wagged its tail joyously. I was blinded by tears, and the vet understood that I had been beaten in my efforts to find the pup a home. He gently guided me to a chair in the corner of the room, and I picked the puppy up and squeezed it fondly. He released it from my grip and firmly assured me that it would take only a few seconds.

Indeed, that is all it took, but those seconds hung heavy on my conscience and I questioned myself what right had I to deprive anything of its life. One minute it was a warm, lively pup and within seconds it was reduced to a cold, stiff carcass. That joyous bark, the swift wag of the tail as it jumped up to greet me, haunted me for days and I swore I would never, never take life again. The fact that it was not by my own hand made me feel no less guilty.

7

A New Environment

Three years of my working life were spent continually in the hills of Simla. I was employed in the offices of the Secretariat which were situated in a valley. The mountain railway passed nearby, Simla being the terminus. A shuttle service ran twice a day, starting from other small stations within a short distance of the lower slopes and this conveniently brought workers up to Simla, from their respective locations further down and conveyed them back down the hill at five o'clock each evening.

On arriving to take up permanent residence in Simla for the duration of my employment, I sought board and lodgings at the local YWCA. It was an imposing building and stood on the summit of a steep hill. Standing in the entrance porch of the YWCA and peering down, one got a bird's eye view of the picturesque Scottish kirk which sheltered in the shadow of our building. Below and beyond, the road branched in two directions. The one on the right stretched downwards along a busy main street lined with shops and restaurants, while the road on the left started up a gradual slope and climbed higher steadily, spreading itself into a square where the library, the Anglican Church and some pretty private dwellings nestled in a partly wooded area.

I often went to this locality as I not only attended the Church but also made a daily visit to a very old lady friend who lived in one of the smaller houses. She was well in her eighties and her only companions were two Airedales. Being unable to walk the dogs herself she was grateful for my visits each evening, to take Brian and Shirl, as she called them, for an outing. I went regularly and the dogs waited impatiently for me at the front door as the hour for my arrival ticked near. She kept their leads hanging from a hook on the wall within their reach, and as I made my appearance at the garden gate Miss Ellie, as my friend was called, would give them a gentle command, "Leads", at which they would immediately take their respective ones off the hook, holding them loosely between their teeth and offering them to me to slip over their heads.

To reach Miss Ellie's house, I had to pass through a wooded patch alive with song birds, chattering monkeys and wood pigeons. A shimmering brook flowed and tumbled down a glade profuse with wild violets and ferns. The brook was spanned by a stout, though delicate-looking wooden bridge, and many a time I was waylaid by a troop of monkeys that would have descended from the trees and taken up position along the railings. Passers-by had cause to be frightened of the monkeys because they were so curious and bold. Always in search of titbits, it was disastrous if you happened to be carrying fruit or food of any kind in an open bag or basket. They immediately attacked the baggage, and it was safer, if alone, to surrender one's wares rather than attempt to beat the animals off. Monkeys imitate man. They pull faces, scratch, yawn and rub their eyes and make chattering noises like some bad-tempered humans, and it is very amusing to watch them, not so much behind bars in a zoo but in their natural habitat.

Simla teemed with monkeys. They were ordinary brown ones, but as one wandered into the thicker and more remote parts of the hills one saw the grey-furred monkeys with black faces. These were more handsome to behold, and their manners were very much more dignified in comparison, for they hardly ever assaulted the passer-by. However, since the brown monkeys were in abundance we remarked their habits more easily.

In the winter months they moved downhill to the warmer plains, though a large number of them remained permanently.

Those that stayed abandoned the snow-covered trees and huddled day and night in groups upon the roofs of the buildings, hugging the chimney stacks for warmth. It amused me to observe them rubbing their paws together in the same way as we did our hands to warm them when they were frozen. They would make regular trips down to the ground to pick up scraps, and then return to the rooftops, and all night long one would hear them crying pitifully as a snow blizzard hit them!

One night, a few days before Christmas, there was a very heavy snowfall, and whilst I got dressed the following morning I glanced out of the bedroom window under which a stout wooden railing wound its way down the sidewalk, and was just in time to witness a most enchanting and almost human incident. Upon the rail sat a baby monkey which no doubt was witnessing its first snowfall and had scooped up a handful of snow and stuck it in its mouth. Immediately, his mother, alongside him, slapped his tiny hand with annoyance, brushed her paw swiftly over his mouth and swept him to her bosom and leapt out of view. I could not help smiling at this amusing spectacle and my mind humorously put her actions into a human mother's words!

When one of their kind dies, the funeral is a long-drawn-out ritual. I witnessed one such occurrence while out hill-climbing with some friends. As we approached what we hoped was our summit, having climbed the slope for a steady two hours or so, we came face-to-face with a massive gathering of monkeys, sitting in orderly fashion in a wide circle. In their midst was their dead companion, and every one of these monkeys was wailing and making a most pathetic cry. Apparently they remain in this fashion for a great length of time, then they lift the dead one further into the forested parts and cover the body completely with leaves.

Life on the hills was much more colourful in comparison to that on the hot, dusty plains. The natural beauty was enthralling and there were four distinct seasons to be observed. There is a lack of these changing scenes on the plains, where the surroundings hardly alter from one year's end to the next, the only changes being in the temperatures which one noticed steadily rising from March until about August when the monsoon broke and caused the temperature to drop slightly.

On the hills the air was clean. One looked fresh and felt refreshed permanently. Recreation was far removed from the man-made form, as the outdoors afforded plenty of opportunity for walking and climbing.

Beauty abounded all round. In just a minute's walk to a pillar box one encountered a shady glade, a silvery waterfall, the scent of wild flowers, the hum of a bee or ducked to allow a pretty butterfly to flit gaily on its way. In the spring, the slopes were a haze of pale pink from the thickly blossoming peach trees and in the winter those same slopes glistened with deep snow.

8

Part 1 ~ No Alternative

One winter's night I had just returned from carol singing. A group of us had spent many hours trudging the snow to spread the joyous news of Christmastide, and it was well after midnight when I prepared for bed. As I nestled between the blankets, grateful for the warmth and comfort of my room, the endless crying of the monkeys on the roof disturbed me.

Suddenly all went quiet. Even the wind quit howling, and it was then, as I was dropping off, that I heard a faint mewing. At first I thought I was dreaming, but the mew turned louder, and peering out of my window I saw, on the ledge of a lower roof which ran along the width of my window, a cat with a kitten in her mouth. What a sad spectacle! There were icicles on her whiskers and the kitten hung cold and limp between her jaws. She made no movement as I leaned over the ledge to lift her up.

This was one time when I threw aside discretion and obedience to the YWCA rules forbidding the encouragement of pets. I put the cat and kitten on a blanket a little distance from the fireside and, with a towel, wiped the cat's fur dry. She immediately started to purr and licked her kitten all over. I had nothing in the way of food or drink to offer the cat, so I crept downstairs and sneaked some milk and a slice of bread from the pantry. I took the chill out of the milk by holding the pan over my fire and then crumbled the bread into the milk, which afforded an excellent snack for Puss. The kitten's eyes were not yet opened, I noticed. Whether she had other kittens elsewhere I never knew, for she did not attempt to get away to fetch any others. Having made the animals as comfortable as I could under the circumstances, I then returned to bed.

In the morning I was faced with a great problem. Should I confide in the other residents or should I not? Whom was I to trust? Not all of them were cat lovers or even animal lovers for that matter. I knew I would have to let it be known to the servant whose duty it was to service my room, and the only way to win his confidence was to bribe him into silence which I did. He proved very helpful when I explained all the details. He vowed not to breathe a word and even obliged by providing a sand tray for the cat, so that she would not be seen climbing in and out of my window. For a time all worked to plan, and I succeeded in keeping my secret from the other residents.

When the kitten was six weeks old, I successfully found it a good home. With the kitten gone I now turned my attention to placing Grey, which was the name I gave the mother cat, prompted by her colouring. She had by now fully accustomed herself to my room and to me, and I was getting very attached to her.

Part 2 ~ Decision

Three months passed, then, one day the very circumstances I feared came to pass. Grey had cleverly pushed the window open, which I had forgetfully left off the catch when leaving for work that morning and was sunning herself happily on the windowsill in full view of the secretary's office across the garden.

The secretary caught sight of this and was furious! She saw, at a glance that Grey was in a healthy condition and appeared much at home in her immediate surroundings, so she realized that the animal was definitely being encouraged as a pet and this made her even more livid. To confirm her suspicion, at this very moment Grey turned around on the sill and re-entered my room. The secretary immediately summoned all the servants before her and cross-questioned them, and threatened with dismissal, the servant, whom I had taken into my confidence, confessed all. I did not hold this against him, however, for it was I who was on trial, not he.

When I returned from work that evening, I found an official note requiring me to report to the secretary's office. She frowned and came straight to the point, reminding me of the rules and giving me twenty-four hours to get rid of Grey. The twenty-four hours having concluded and the situation unaltered, she made a formal complaint against me to the Board of Management. With a haste that a crisis would warrant, the entire Board, which was composed of about ten members, met, and I was summoned to their presence.

The atmosphere and even the form in which our seating arrangements were placed represented a miniature courtroom. My jury sat in a semicircle at one end of the long boardroom and I upon a straight-backed chair, a distance of a few yards away, facing the firing line. The president, who was the local vicar's wife, cross-questioned and hammered explanations out of me as though I had committed a monstrous crime. Instead of a pat on my back for the compassion I had showed to an animal in distress, I was rebuked, and the authorities offered me the choice of either getting rid of the cat by the morning or leaving. As this pronouncement was delivered, a long loud "Meow" pierced the air, and to my surprise, Grey strode through the open door, down the length of the room and straight to me, oblivious of all. There was a hush as I picked her up, announced my decision to leave first thing in the morning and bade my jury farewell.

I hurried upstairs to my room, packed my belongings and later went to my friends, the Lamons, and informed them that they had a guest arriving in the morning, accompanied by pet, whether they liked it or not! Needless to say, they liked it, for I was always a welcome guest at their home and they immediately set about preparing the spare room for me and Grey. Thus ended my stay at that particular YWCA though, bearing no malice, I continued to keep in close touch with its activities. I just hoped that in upholding my principle of not abandoning a dumb creature under any circumstances, I proved in some small way my recognition of God's creatures and drove home to those well-meaning ladies that one cannot run a Christian organization if the very act of doing a kind deed is censured.

Part 3 ~ Reward

As time passed, Grey amply rewarded me for the consideration I had shown her by cautioning me of extreme dangers that I was not aware of at times. Hot countries crawl with snakes, scorpions and other gruesome insects, all unpleasant to encounter and quite a number of them very dangerous.

One morning, as I prepared to get dressed, I noticed that Grey had taken root under my bed. She sat perfectly still with her eyes widened and a fixed gaze at the space under my wardrobe, which stood about two feet away from the bed and four inches off the floor. From sheer curiosity and not anticipating any danger, I climbed down on my knees to detect what it was that held her gaze for so long, disregarding even my offer of her morning meal which, at other times, she was impatient for.

It was dark under the wardrobe and I could see nothing, but after a full half-hour, as she was still frozen in her position, I was determined to appease my curiosity. I shone my torch under the wardrobe, at the same time kneeling down, and in the beam of light I was horrified to spy a huge black scorpion. I shuddered when I remembered how, only a little while ago, I had stood about in open slippers by my wardrobe, and it was only Grey's concentrated gaze, I imagined, that had mesmerised the scorpion into immobility. A sting from this deadly species would have proved fatal.

Leaving her still in control, I quickly left the room and called for help. We successfully killed the scorpion, and I remained ever grateful to Grey.

Summer and autumn passed by and once again winter was upon us. One night whilst I slept peacefully, with Grey warmly curled up in a chair by my bedside, the end of my eiderdown had slipped carelessly and it fell within reach of the electric fire. An inch or two had smouldered and Grey was quick to sense the danger. Through my deep sleep I felt a persistent pawing at my face, and she finally succeeded in arousing me and thus saved a disaster.

Early in the spring of the next year my friends, the Lamons, were transferring from Simla down to the Nilgiris. It meant my looking for new accommodation, but I had no difficulty, as an offer to stay with them came spontaneously from another good friend of mine. She was a spinster and kept home for her aged mother. They were fond of dogs and had four terriers. How Grey was going to cope with this I had no idea, but I was to devise a satisfactory arrangement for keeping the peace.

The room I used opened out on to the side of the house and there was a large window along one end. The exit from this window escaped into a plot of garden which was conveniently fenced off, and this barrier prevented the dogs from reaching Grey. However, if we were all to live united and Grey to enjoy the fireside and our company in the drawing room on cold nights, we decided that an effort to get the animals to be friends must be persevered with.

Accordingly, I carried Grey into the dogs' presence for a few minutes each day. Their first reaction was alarming as all four yapped and barked and almost bowled me over. Grey trembled and growled and hissed bad-temperedly, at the same time digging her claws deep into my arm and drawing blood as she swished her tail angrily. This first attempt to introduce her to the dogs was abandoned within seconds, but we did not despair and I repeatedly carried her into the drawing room each night.

At the end of a week or so, the dogs suddenly accepted her, and though she growled a bit in response she actually remained on in the room. From then on, there was no more aggression and all became good friends. Occasionally she would arch her back and hiss if one of the dogs moved towards her, but even this distrust of them gradually faded.

In the summer of that year Grey once again made herself responsible for my safety. I had been out dancing, arriving home well after midnight, and Grey was in the room when I snapped on the light. Tired from a hectic party, I yawned, kicked off my dancing shoes and slipped out of my dress. Grey still sat motionless, her gaze upon the floor in the direction of my bedside table. I flopped into the nearby chair and stretched out my hand to pat her, but she would not be distracted. Playfully I chided her for being unsociable and, still in frivolous mood, I fetched her ball and rolled it gently in her direction.

The unexpected movement of the ball caused her to leap in the air and land on my bed. Her eyes stared excitedly and she looked terrified. Simultaneously, as she leapt from the fright I had given her, I saw something move under the bedside table. It resembled, in that split second, the flex from the table lamp, and I bent to steady it, but leapt back in terror when I recognized it to be a snake!

This is what Grey had been guarding for how many hours previous to my returning home I shall never know. I jumped upon the bed beside her and screamed for help. My shouts started the four terriers barking and my friend Kay rushed to me from her bedroom on the other side of the house.

The snake did not get away. It lay perfectly still along the side of the wall and Kay attacked it with a small hatchet, the first weapon she lay her hands on in her haste to get something with which to kill the reptile. I was in a state of shock, and on examining the remains, we discovered it was a krait – a deadly Indian rock snake whose bite I should never have survived.

Part 4 ~ A Family Condemned

Periodically, Grey entered into the usual courtships with eligible toms that offered their attentions and had already twice had a litter of three kittens a time, involving me in the usual difficulties of finding good homes for them.

Now, in the early hours of one morning, I was awakened by Grey pawing me and mewing gently. She led me to understand that the event was about to take place yet again, and took up her position in the spacious cardboard box I had specially prepared for her. Sleepily, I walked over to the box where she lay and gently stroked her brow as she laboured and gave birth to one – two – three – four kittens! The first two were like her, the third as shiny and black as ebony and the last one was ginger. She licked and nursed them with great tenderness, purring continuously. I offered her some warm milk which she lapped up gratefully. With her family now clean and complete, she suckled them all into her fur and allowed me to return to bed.

On the household awakening, I announced the good news, and Kay and her mother were delighted and immediately made for my room to see the family. Now, cats are very intelligent and extremely independent. They make their own decisions and invite a human to either like it, or not. They do not believe in making themselves look ridiculous and because it is never guaranteed that a cat will obey a command in the same way as a dog does, people who do not understand cats pronounce them stupid and believe them to be ignorant of the spoken word. I know from long experience, however, that this is not true. I used to conduct long, intelligent conversations with Grey who replied aptly in different tones of mews and by the use of her tail. So, whilst we were collected around her, exclaiming over the kittens, how pained and appalled she must have been when my friend Kay blurted out, 'Three of them will have to go!'

I did not know what had possessed her to make this decision and the suggestion threw me off balance.

She continued, not unkindly, but in a firm practical tone, 'We'll keep one for Grey – the others we'll destroy.'

'Indeed!' I thought. 'Which one of us is to do this ghastly deed? And in what way are we to decide which three are to forfeit life?'

I was haunted with visions of how I had sat up with Grey in the earlier hours of the morning, witnessing her pain and strain as she had given birth, proud of her efforts when the act had been accomplished. I felt sick at heart and said no more.

'I'll look in at the hospital for some chloroform on my way home from work,' Kay went on. 'A sniff through cotton wool and the kittens would soon be out – painlessly.'

I knew that the Matron of the local hospital would oblige with the chloroform as she was a personal friend of Kay's, but I was not having any part in this mass murder. Since Grey and I were indebted for our accommodation, there was little I could do to insist on keeping Grey's family alive and complete, if our hostess wished otherwise, but I explained that this act of destroying the kittens had best be carried out in my absence whilst I was away at the office. Therefore, it was agreed that Kay would take the afternoon off to execute the deed and heavy-hearted I left for work.

Kay did just as she had said. She finished work at one that afternoon, armed herself with the chloroform and arrived home. My room was left unlocked and the window slightly open to allow Grey the access of coming and going. Kay entered my room to remove three of the kittens to the bathroom, where she was to execute these tiny lives. Then she stood aghast for the cardboard box was empty! Grey and all four kittens had vanished. Kay called loudly to Grey and searched the garden, but there was no sign of her anywhere.

As I wended my way wearily back from work at the end of the day, I wondered how I was going to face Grey and which kitten would be the lucky one that had been chosen to live on. However, as I came to the front door, Kay met me with the news of Grey's disappearance. I was alarmed, but, at the same time, secretly happy to learn of the escape. I knew that Grey would manage to care for her family wherever she had fled to, as she had proved to be a good mother on past occasions. I spent many hours that evening, wandering the grounds in search of her. I called her name and slid up and down the hill slopes which enveloped the house, but Grey never showed up. Days multiplied into weeks and my sorrow was great.

It is customary for a cat to change her kittens about from place to place and Grey had often done so with past litters, but had restricted these transfers only from one side of the room to the other or from one room to the next. Never, at any time, did she move kittens to the outdoors as she had now done, and her action gave me food for thought.

Four weeks later, on a Sunday afternoon, we were lazing around after lunch when Kay stood up and walked across the room to the window. Immediately, she turned back and beckoned me to her side.

'Look at that!' she exclaimed, pointing to an object climbing down the hillside which rose a little distance from the house.

I peered and could not believe my eyes, for the moving object was Grey. She was treading downwards slowly and assuredly, and a few seconds later we caught sight of one shiny jet object, two grey and a ginger blob following in her trail. I shouted with joy and made for the door, and Kay and I hurried up to the furry line winding its way down. Grey mewed softly and rubbed herself against my legs, and the kittens assembled about us unafraid and mewed in a chorus. We noticed they had been well cared for. Their coats were clean and shiny, but Grey herself looked very lean, tired and a trifle scruffy. I picked her up and she was as light as a feather. She needed a good meal. Kay gathered up the kittens before the dogs bounded out to see what we had found, and on returning to the house we locked them all safely in my room. I quickly offered saucers of milk to the kittens, and for Grey there was a special saucer of raw meat chopped up finely. How she relished it!

Having eaten, the adorable family circulated about my room, licking their whiskers, faces and paws clean. Grey supervised a little of their grooming, but there was not the usual fussing that a mother cat gives to her very young. She knew that they had outgrown that close supervision.

What a joyous ending this was for me after the weeks of anxiety and heartbreak I had silently endured over Grey's mysterious disappearance. That night I chose to read the passage in the New Testament that tells of Herod's wicked instructions to kill all male children under the age of two, in his pursuit to destroy the Christ Child, resulting in a general exodus as mothers fled for the safety of their young. The story seemed to identify itself with Grey's behaviour. Mother love bore its pressure when she had heard Kay's outrageous suggestion to do away with her tiny mites, and from this particular incident I became even more assured of cats' intelligence and understanding of human speech.

It did not take long to find homes for the kittens. Meanwhile for the short period that they were with us they delighted us with their frolics. Grey once again settled into the normal routine and renewed her friendship with the dogs, who welcomed her back into their midst. She never again went further than the immediate boundaries of the garden.

Part 5 ~ Adversity

Cruelty raises its ugly head within the animal kingdom too, and this I bitterly experienced in the winter of that year. It had snowed continuously and this hazard presented difficulties to the wild animals that usually kept to the higher peaks. In their search for food, some took courage and wandered downwards to the inhabited places. Reports in the local newspaper about the odd wild animal having been spotted or shot here and there did not hold my attention unduly, for it was generally accepted that the spot where we lived, though sparsely populated, was a little too low in the valley to attract wild beasts. Our complacence in this belief was soon shattered, however.

It was just seven o'clock, and the evening was pitch dark. Grey asked to be allowed out as she did each night, stopping out for a few minutes and promptly returning to the comfort and safety of the indoors for the rest of the night. As I opened the door, an icy draught froze my face and hands and a deathly quiet reigned. She slipped out and I saw a great black object pounce upon her and speed up the hillside, carrying her off in its savage jaws!

A couple of days later we read in the newspaper that a panther had been shot in our area. It had, in that short period, taken four household pets, and one of them was my beloved Grey.

Hearts mend, but scars remain, and memories of Grey stayed with me constantly and lurked about my room. It was difficult to attend to my work, to meet friends and make light chatter. Therefore, three months later, when I was informed of my transfer back to my headquarters in the plains of Delhi, I received the news without much regret.

As I journeyed down the hills I knew that I would never return, but a small part of me remained behind on those slopes, now alive with spring blossom.

9

Part 1 ~ A Voyage

The bustling noise and crowds of Delhi soon dispersed all sentiment. The tempo at which life moved rocketed me out of my grief and proved a tonic. During the three years of my absence from these parts, most of my old friends had left. India had changed politically in the past three years inasmuch as she had gained her independence now, and with its arrival many of my British friends had returned to the UK. Other locally-born friends were making plans, too, for burning their bridges and emigrating to Britain, Australia and Canada. So I found I had very few old acquaintances left and I set about acquiring new associations. This was not difficult as I was now back in the YWCA and became thoroughly involved in all its activities. Doubtless, I still continued to help the lame dog over the stile in my spare moments, but I never took it upon myself to break another YWCA rule!

Life moved along with interest for a few months and then I suddenly became disheartened. I imagined I was allowing myself to get into a rut, although I was never short of male admirers or of invitations to parties and dances. I took a very active part in social services such as organizing a youth club, helping in a local leper colony, contributing towards the Church choir and generally making myself useful. Even so, I felt that life was passing me by, and the temptation to do something really spectacular became a burning desire. I had not, however, the wherewithal to achieve this and disappointment lay heavy. I envied my girlfriends with rich parents who packed them off to foreign countries or those girls who threw loyalties to the winds, scooped together all they had and bought a one-way ticket to somewhere else. I often hoped I had the courage to follow suit, but could have rested assured if I had believed in the saying, "Every dog shall have its day."

Certainly, mine came when I least expected it, quite out of the blue. My lucky star hit me hard and on target, for overnight I became a successful applicant to an appointment which was going to take me on a wonderful journey through Europe, to conclude finally in South America.

I could not believe this had happened to me as I went about starry-eyed, arranging for my travel documents, saying hurried farewells to my friends, informing my mother and relatives of my sudden departure and absolutely bewildered with the uncertainty of entering the unknown.

I had been chosen out of three hundred applicants to join a South American diplomat's family as the English tutor for their young daughter and son. They had completed their tour in India and were now returning to the Argentine. En route, we were to holiday in Europe, then board another liner and head for the New World. What was there to say but drop on my knees and thank God for His goodness?

India is a vast country, and a journey to the coast would have involved several days and great expense. Our hometown had been tucked inland, therefore I had never seen the sea. During my working years, after leaving home, though I had journeyed the length of India, from almost the southern tip to well into the Himalayas, these journeys had run perpendicularly through the centre of the country, and so the sea remained a mystery. Now, for the first time in my twenty-five years of life, I was going to set eyes upon it. Not only set eyes, but delve through miles and miles of it for days and days. This was only one of the many wonderful sights that became mine.

My friends held farewell parties for me and endowed me with gifts to remember them by. I went around taking snapshots of old places and old faces that I never expected to see again, and I rushed my rolls of film to the local photographer to have them developed before leaving India.

The photographer's shop was not more than a hovel with mud-plastered walls, but I was informed that the results of his work were always satisfactory and that he did not charge as much as the more notable photographers in the town itself. I entered the shop, which was empty except for a large fluffy black and white cat that sat composedly on the counter. I tickled her chin, and she purred and rubbed her whiskers along my hand. It was as she stood up to her full height that I saw she had no tail! Only a small stump of fur took the place of what should have been, in her breed, a thick flowing brush. This was ridiculous and I wondered how the poor creature had met her accident.

A cat's tail spells out a language of its own when cat meets cat, and it is used as a balancing rudder. Different movements of the tail express the various feelings and conditions of a cat. Whether it be a long, slim tail, short, thick tail, or a tapering one, the owner is equally proud of it and would be completely lost without it, except the Manx, of course, which seems to manage without one.

As I mused, the owner of the shop made his appearance through a side door and greeted me with a wide smile, but completely distracted by the cat without her tail, I departed from the main purport of my visit and immediately fired him with my question, 'What happened to the cat's tail?'

He looked taken aback but still smiled as he apologetically replied, 'We cut it off.'

'Whatever for?' I demanded.

Still in apologetic good humour, he continued, 'When the animal was very small we found it in a bush. We thought it was a dog. Therefore, we cut its tail. But as it grew older it began to miaow and it is only then we realized that it was a cat and not a dog.'

Concluding his story, he still grinned all over his face as he awaited my further comment.

If I had not seen and heard this sorry tale for myself, I would never have believed it to be true. This was ignorance at its height. It was also my last connections with the animal world in India before I set out on my unforgettable journey to strange-sounding places.

Part 2 ~ The Sea

Within ten days of my being offered the position, we left Delhi by train for Bombay, from which port we were to embark on our liner, the *Oceania*. She was doing her maiden voyage and was homeward bound from Australia to Genoa. We were travelling first class and the passenger list was made up of dignitaries. The thrill and splendour of a luxury liner took my breath away, and I paced her decks with the excitement of a child.

My cabin adjoined the children's, but for most of the voyage I was relieved of many duties, leaving them in the care of the ship's nurse, and I took part in all the entertainment provided. The cuisine spelt delicacy at every meal and I became thoroughly acquainted with the Italian farinacci, which was something new to my palate, having always been accustomed to English or Indian food. It intrigued me to watch my table steward manipulate the spaghetti with such ease, and I asked him to give me my first lesson on how to attack it. By the end of the voyage I was an expert at handling it and no longer slipped it all over the tablecloth or, from exasperation, chopped it into pieces and scooped it up with a spoon.

The sea needs some comment. As I have said, I had never set eyes on it before, and when I did it brought a lump to my throat. We set sail at one o'clock, having embarked at ten that morning, and the excitement of getting aboard, exploring my cabin with its magic buttons that moved the furniture around, changing the space from lounge to bedroom and back, and getting attuned to the foreign tongues about me, made me, at first, disregard the very existence of the watery base we floated upon.

The ship's band played a lively tune, the gangplank was up and friends and spectators on the quayside waved and we threw our streamers out to them. The spirit of carnival spread on deck as the stewards distributed party hats, masks and whistles, and unnoticeably, the *Oceania* had glided into the Indian Ocean.

I realized that the buildings on the horizon were receding into a background of very blue skies. The gigantic stone structure of the Gateway of India shrank and it was then that I came to earth. My eyes filled and the tears spilled, my throat went dry and an awful pain tugged at my inside. I looked over the side of the ship and ahead, and all I saw was a shimmering green, which took my breath away with its beauty and vastness. It represented volumes of space that now divided me from the unknown and the only land, a mere speck by now, that I knew and loved. The loneliness of the water, thousands of miles of it about me, made me feel small and insignificant, and I stood for a long time watching the waves break past as the *Oceania* ripped them apart.

Later on, I mingled with the other passengers and found them to be mainly Italian, Spanish and French. There were only two Indian families, also of diplomatic standing. Being a brunette with an olive complexion, I was easily mistaken for Italian or Spanish nationality and was promptly referred to as "Senorita" or "Signorina".

Once we had left the shores of Bombay, I hardly heard the English language. The entire crew was Italian and my cabin steward, table steward and even the ship's officers addressed me in Italian, taking for granted that I could be nothing else. I had quickly to enlighten them of my true origin but, in order to circulate freely, I felt that the language barrier must be overcome, so I picked up words and phrases of Italian and Spanish which I practised diligently.

Part 3 ~ An Encounter

On the first evening of the voyage and having experienced my first glorious sight of a sunset at sea, I began to feel the pangs of homesickness. The glamour of the ballroom, all the wining and dining and superb music, could not help me forget my homeland and loved ones. So, breaking away from the immediate fun that all the others appeared to be revelling in, I disappeared along the deck and up a flight of stairs to the top deck.

The *Oceania* had a myriad of coloured fairy lights picking out her form and must have looked an exquisite picture from afar in the inky darkness of the sea. I climbed still another flight of stairs and found myself on the uppermost deck. It was quiet, and a gentle breeze swished the folds of my long evening dress. There was not a soul in sight and I could hear, faintly, the melody of a dance number. It was eleven o'clock.

As I strolled along the promenade I suddenly came upon a large, comfortable cage, with shiny silver bars and upholstered in pale blue quilted satin. It was firmly secured and rested upon an iron extension of the ship, about four to five feet off the deck. I moved closer and found, to my delight, a creature of sheer beauty. It was a Persian with soft flowing silky hair. She reposed, as Persians tend to, in a most indolent fashion. I poked a finger through the bars to stroke her fur and pampered her with caressing words, and she loved every minute of it. I saw a silver nameplate screwed upon one side of the cage, and in the dim light rhinestones glittered the name "Samantha".

All the sadness I felt suddenly left me and I stayed for a while enjoying my new company. I told no one of my discovery, and at different times of the following days I sneaked up to see her. It was obvious that she belonged to one of the passengers and I noticed that she did not travel permanently on that secluded part of the ship, for her owners, whom I later found to be an Italian count and countess bound for Naples, tended her carefully and often transferred her to their cabin for feeding and grooming.

Part 4 ~ Seeing the World

On the fourth day we arrived at Aden. It was seven o'clock in the morning when we dropped anchor. The ship stopped about six or seven miles out to sea, and at nine o'clock we were allowed to go ashore. Motor launches came alongside and for a small charge sped us to the land. We found Aden to be a large port, but very barren, for there was not a tree or blade of grass to be seen. The heat was intense and the only enjoyment we derived was from stretching our legs on Mother Earth once more. We strolled along the shopping area and spent a lot of money stocking up with English woollies and nylon stockings which were remarkably cheap.

At four o'clock that afternoon we again set sail, and ploughed our way through the Red Sea, which was so hot that it looked like boiling water and doubtless felt like it.

Three days later we reached Suez, and after a day's pleasant and interesting cruising up the Suez Canal we arrived at Port Said. From then on we voyaged in the Mediterranean, where there was a distinct change in temperature and weather conditions.

A few hours after entering the Mediterranean, I went up to see Samantha. Imagine my horror to find her stretched out in an alarming fashion and frothing at the mouth. The first conclusion, that she had been poisoned, raced through my mind, and I rushed for help.

As I sped along the deck, in my hurry and despair I stumbled straight into the arms of one of the ship's officers. I apologised, and he smiled and raised his hand politely to the peak of his hat. I stared at him in terror and, pointing in the direction of Samantha's cage, I quickly blurted, 'The cat – someone has poisoned her – She's frothing at the mouth!'

My gesticulations and rapid flow of the English language confused him, and he invited me to explain myself again. This was hopeless, I thought. I could not waste time. So I dragged him by the arm and led him to the scene.

On seeing Samantha's condition, however, he threw back his head and exploded with laughter. I looked at him in astonishment and anger, but as I made off to call for other help he held me back and controlled his mirth. He explained, in very broken English, seeing that I had not understood his spontaneous remarks in Italian, that Samantha was only seasick! A cat, he further informed me, was a very good indicator to bad weather, as a cat on board always felt the effects of seasickness twenty-four hours before a storm. There must have been some truth in what he said, for though at that given moment the Mediterranean was as serene as a fish tank, it certainly belched up a tremendous storm twenty-four hours later!

The *Oceania* boasted stabilisers. All the same, it tossed like an eggshell upon the angry sea. The waves were a menacing grey and hit well above the decks, and I was confined to my cabin overtaken by a malady I had had no experience of. It was a horrible sinking feeling, and my head seemed to be disjointed from the rest of my body. The cabin, so solid and secure, creaked and groaned, the ceiling appeared to be falling lower and lower and at the same time the floor rose higher. I knew what Samantha must have felt! This, my first experience of seasickness, lasted for many hours, and it was not likely to be my last because thousands of miles of ocean were still to be crossed and I dreaded the remainder of the voyage.

The storm having passed, we sailed on, enjoying the beauty of a serene sea. I had fully recovered and so had Samantha. We passed the island of Crete late one evening and the entire mass of land was alight, resembling some enchanting fairyland. Later that same night, we sailed under the nose of Stromboli, the famous volcanic mountain.

The following day we entered the Straits of Messina and at six o'clock we wound our way round the Isle of Capri. Its hillsides were a blaze of colour, from the masses of bright flowers that grew in wild profusion. A picture to behold! And this was in winter. As we moved around the isle, we got a view of Naples and reached it by seven-thirty that morning. We breakfasted and then went ashore, spending the morning sightseeing and returning to the ship for lunch. Then a party of us set out to visit Pompeii. The weather was fine, and for three short hours we roamed the ruins of the city, living the story with the help of a guide.

A visit to Vesuvius was also possible and we thoroughly enjoyed its wondrous beauty and unexpected thrills. With the assistance of the guide we descended into the interior of the crater. Of particular interest were the remains of lava streams of past eruptions and the striking colours and deformations assumed by the solidified lava.

On returning to our ship late that night, I felt a small pang of loneliness, for Samantha was no longer aboard. Her owners had been met ceremoniously that morning when we docked, and as she was carried down the gangplank I bade her goodbye.

The *Oceania* once more set sail, and we disembarked in Genoa the following afternoon. Officials from the Embassy met us with a certain amount of grandeur and we were escorted to the Columbia Hotel. A few days later, as my employers had to attend to business in France, I chose not to remain on in the hotel during their long absence, so they arranged for me to move into the Villa Teresita. The villa was tucked away in the mountains of St Ilario, about twenty miles from the town, and it was picturesque, tiny and with every modern convenience. There were only three other residents; in fact, that was all the villa would accommodate. It was run by two nuns but, though I had every comfort, I was extremely lonely since neither of the nuns, nor the other residents, understood or spoke a word of English, and I strove desperately to make conversation through a small English-Italian dictionary that I carried with me constantly.

Each morning after breakfast I set out on a walk to admire the panorama and to explore the beauties of the Perla del Golfo Paradiso, as Nervi is called. On other occasions I boarded a local bus which wended its way down to the village that spread itself out at the foot of the hills. I battled with my attempts at shopping for toilet requisites and souvenirs. I completely baffled the village shopkeepers by my foreign tongue.

The only way I overcame my loneliness, caused by the language barrier, was by diverting my attention towards the various cats I passed, sitting contentedly upon the garden walls or fences. The language of love needs no words and this theory applies also when communicating with God's dumb creatures. A caress, a pat on the head and a soft tone of voice soon establishes a friendship, and I knew that I could talk sweet words to my heart's content to the soft, furry tabby upon the wall and that her response would prove interesting and entertaining.

By taking these daily walks along the same route, I soon got to learn to which house each cat belonged. Stopping to stroke a pet inevitably invited comment from the householder, and though I could not continue further than just the odd word or two of Italian, at least some tiny bit of communication had taken place.

Part 5 ~ Animal Devotion

Not far from the villa was a small Catholic cathedral. It perched precariously upon a ledge on the mountainside and its restricted boundaries boasted a few gravestones which sheltered under some picturesque trees. I often strolled past the churchyard to a bench, situated a little beyond, where I loved to sit in solitude and read or write letters.

One day, whilst thus occupied, my eyes strayed from my book and towards the gravestones. There, upon a mound devoid of tombstone, I saw a large sheep dog stretched out to his full length, with his head resting between his front paws, I noticed there was no one with him and wondered where he had come from. On various occasions after that, when I made my way to my favourite refuge, I caught sight of this same animal, and one morning, plucking up courage, I made towards him. As I approached, the only movement he volunteered was with his large brown eyes which cautiously searched me, and when I uttered a few words to him his tail stirred very slowly. I tried to attract him away from the grave by offering him a biscuit, but could not succeed. For days I remained curiously eager to have an explanation of this animal's behaviour but, being unable to relate the incident to anyone, I could not find my answer.

On the eve of my leaving the villa, however, I was making a last trip to the village and since the journey down the hill took a full half-hour, I decided to make a note of all the things I needed to do in the village. Accordingly, I pulled out my notebook and pencil from my handbag and began writing. Beside me sat a young, fashionable Italian girl. Whilst I scribbled hurriedly, her eyes turned downwards and I realized that she was reading my notes. All at once, she exclaimed, 'You are English?'

I was so taken aback to hear these few words in my own language, after spending almost three weeks amid a foreign din, that I replied excitedly, 'Yes. Are you?'

'No, Miss,' she answered. 'I am Italian, but I speak a little of English.'

She knew sufficient for me to hold an interesting conversation and, still eager to know the answer, I ventured, 'Do you know the churchyard near Villa Teresita?'

'Yes,' she responded.

I then told her about the dog I had seen there regularly and asked if she knew anything about it.

She held my interest by explaining that the dog had belonged to an old shepherd who had died a few weeks previously at the age of ninety. The dog had been his companion for the past ten years, leading him in his blindness. On his death, the relatives took the pet to the funeral and since then it was impossible to keep the animal at home, for at the first opportunity he ran back to the graveside and refused to leave. They had made several attempts to take him back to the house but, on securing him, he whined and howled alarmingly and refused all food. In order not to cause the animal distress, the relatives therefore allowed him his freedom, and apparently he stayed at the graveside constantly, his owners taking him his meals daily.

'Fidelity in every sense of the word!' I uttered.

'Fi- ?' she attempted, with an inquiring look in her dark eyes.

'Fi-del-i-ti,' I repeated, pronouncing each syllable.

'Fi-del-i-ti,' she echoed. 'What does it mean?'

I gave her a brief explanation of the word and she seemed overjoyed with this addition to her limited vocabulary.

She kept repeating the word to herself, and while she thus recited it with almost a musical air, my mind's eye conjured up warm thoughts for the animal, so endowed by God with a keen sense of faithfulness that would put to shame the lack of devotion some humans show to one another.

10

Part 1 ~ Beyond the Equator

The following day, I left the villa and returned to the Columbia Hotel in Genoa to be reunited with my employers who had returned from their wanderings. We had a great deal of news to exchange over the three weeks of separation and I amused them with my tales of the difficulties I had encountered over the language barrier.

At the end of the week, we boarded the *Conte Biancamano* and set sail for the Argentine. As in the *Oceania*, the passenger list again sported the names of the wealthy and famous. The English language, by now, was something completely unknown, Spanish, Portuguese, Italian and a spattering of French being the media used, and I was getting trained to these sounds. The *Conte Biancamano* was even bigger than the *Oceania* and I still gasped with delight at the splendour of all things aboard.

We called at Villafranca the same day we set sail and the following day we stopped at Barcelona. Having an entire day ashore gave us the opportunity to see all the magnificent sights that this city had to offer, and we made the most of this outing because we knew that once we set sail again it would be five or six days of continuous sailing before we would sight land.

We left Barcelona late in the evening, and for the rest of the following day sailed along the Spanish coast, then entered the Straits of Gibraltar. The sea was very choppy, and once again I kept to my cabin with seasickness. Once we left the Straits it was comparatively calmer, and for the next day or two the coast of Africa was visible. After the five long days at sea we welcomed the stop at Dakar. It was late evening when we docked and fleets of taxis were available for us to visit inland. The taxi-drivers looked a strange sight in whiter than white robes which flowed down to their ankles. In the inky darkness of the night and the subdued lighting at the port, they looked like a multitude of ghosts as they raced towards us, inviting us to use this taxi and that. Their dark-skinned faces were completely indiscernible and only a solid white gash gleamed somewhere between a blob of white headdress and the commencement of the long white flowing robe. Taxi after taxi sped along in the darkness and, after some time, the bright lights of the town centre blinded us. Music boomed from every building, and there was plenty of nightlife to revel in.

We returned to our ship at about three o'clock completely exhausted after a hectic night out. We left Dakar at dawn and during the following week, whilst we were tossed in the Atlantic Ocean, I took to my cabin once more with attacks of seasickness.

It was very, very hot as we neared the Equator, and the usual welcoming aboard of Father Neptune took place as we crossed the line. All the passengers assembled around the large swimming pool for the fun and games that included every one of us, and it proved a hilarious afternoon. The ocean was calm and the skies a bright blue. The sun scorched and we sweated even in our brief swim suits. That night there was a grand Fancy Dress Ball.

After a few more days at sea we caught a superb view of Rio de Janeiro with the El Christo statue projecting into the azure sky, welcoming us with outstretched arms, from the tip of the Pao de Acucar. We docked for a day and, it being the middle of summer, it was ideal to join the Brazilian crowds on the Copacabana beach.

From Rio we sailed to the smaller port of Santos. We went ashore, but the only memory I have of this seaport is of the enormous and numerous crabs that crawled and toddled everywhere in regiments. The row of tiny shops laden with the local wares were, I noticed, built on wooden platforms which stood a foot or so off the ground. And no wonder, for the moving carpets of crabs seemed to be everywhere and fitted tightly together in the space on the ground under these wooden platforms. They ran and crawled in all directions and it was impossible to stand at ease and do the shopping. I screamed in terror and fled up the cobbled road to get away from this area, but was horrified to find that an army of crabs was marching straight at me from the opposite direction along the cobbled pavement that I was on. I gave up, and retraced my steps to the safety of the ship.

After Santos, we sailed on through the night, disembarking at Montevideo around noon the following day. Montevideo is a magnificent harbour with smart white buildings, and the first beach one comes upon is Pocitos. Arising out of it was the imposing Rambla Hotel, a multi-storeyed structure, and we were booked into a suite of rooms on the eleventh floor.

Having rested for a day or two, we then took a night boat to Buenos Aires where we were to spend Christmas and the New Year at the family home of my employers. It proved both an exciting and sad experience, as memories of past Christmases at home haunted me. However, I endeavoured to appreciate this new experience in the midst of the splendour and wealth that seemed to surround me.

The family's home turned out to be a luxurious mansion occupying a large part of a select avenue. Christmas fare overspilled, the house rocked with merriment and household servants tripped over each other. With what grandeur the turkey was carved on its solid silver salver, and the champagne glasses raised! Outside, the town glowed with Christmas trees along its pavements and the shops buzzed with life. Life that never ceased, for shops never closed. They remained open day and night, shop assistants working shifts to permit this convenience to shoppers who, having forgotten a gift or an essential in the day's rush, could nip out, whatever the time, to purchase their requirement.

The local inhabitants contributed to the gaiety of the scene. It being the height of summer, they were clad in the minimum – girls in scanty swimsuits and beachwear and the men in very colourful shirts, very short shorts and large coloured sombreros.

Christmas is generally spent on the beaches or under the cool palms. Most people, at least the ones that I came in contact with, owned private aeroplanes and visited their friends in them, and it astonished me to see "Air Park" notices as commonly displayed as the less glamorous "Car Park" or "Cycle Stand" that I had seen in the countries I had previously passed through. We spent a hectic Christmas season, shopping all day and celebrating with house parties and dances at night.

Soon after the New Year, we caught the night steamer back to Uruguay where we were to remain permanently for at least a year, and my employers bought a new house in the most fashionable part of Montevideo. We all felt happy at the thought of unpacking our boxes for that last time. The locality was paved with wealth and every household in the vicinity kept a small battalion of domestic servants. There was plenty for me to see and do as I tried to fit into the way of life that now faced me.

The children were settled into a private day school and this left me at a loose end from nine in the morning until four in the afternoon. The language barrier rendered me lonesome, and it was decided that if I were to overcome this hurdle and get accustomed to the people around me I should learn the language. Therefore, arrangements were made for a Spanish professor to visit me daily at the house and I devoted the entire morning, until lunch, to my studies.

Three months of this routine soon passed, and the lessons were helping me enormously. I could read and write Spanish fairly well by this time. The sounds that were gibberish to me in the past suddenly became meaningful and I began to understand more readily the street signs, advertisements and newspaper headlines. Armed with so much knowledge of the Spanish language, I now had the confidence to make friends, to go shopping alone, to make appointments with the hairdresser and even hop on a streetcar and get the thrill of asking for a ticket to here and there, instead of resorting to the family car chaperoned by the chauffeur. I obtained membership at the local clubs for dancing, musical concerts and opera, boating and amateur dramatics. I even joined the exclusive Montevideo Cricket Club where gay dances and dinners were held each Saturday night for its members.

I was well on the road to becoming fully acquainted with the social life of Montevideo.

Part 2 ~ A Sudden Change

Just as I was making such tremendous strides towards getting to know the country and my environments, however, my employer unexpectedly received orders to leave for the United States, and so, having spent only three months instead of the twelve that they had hoped to enjoy in Montevideo, they began their packing once more. But I had decided against moving out of South America and accordingly resigned my position, taking up another with a well-known Uruguayan family. Their home, too, was situated in a very select part of the town and sprawled down half the length of a shady avenue. I was employed as the English teacher for their children and was provided with comfortable living quarters in the grandfather's property, which was situated on an avenue a few minutes walk away. In fact, my accommodation amounted to a roomy cottage which stood in the private grounds belonging to the family.

The grandfather's house was a magnificent building of typical Spanish architecture. The courtyard was tiled with mosaic and an ornate garden surrounded the house. In passing through the tall front gates, a distance of ten yards led to a wrought iron gate which curtained the imposing entrance to the house itself. Set a couple of yards beyond this gate was a solid oak door. This opened out into a wide oblong hall and visitors could leave their coats and hats in the cloakrooms which were immediately to the left and right of the hall. At the far end, a wide staircase ascended to a square landing over the hall, from which opened a dozen large bedrooms. There was a bathroom to every two rooms, carried out in the same colour as the rooms and furnishings. The eighth and ninth rooms detached themselves to allow a short flight of stairs to a long passage which ended in the family's private chapel. It was spacious enough to hold eighteen persons, the altar was continually alight with candles and a solid gold crucifix adorned the centre. Family prayers were held regularly there each day.

Beyond the chapel there was a turning, and a further short staircase led up to a long, bright sewing room where two needlewomen attended to the household sewing. They could enter and leave the house by a back staircase which wended its way down to the servants' entrance by the side of the house.

The dining and breakfast rooms stretched down along one side of the entrance hall, their latticed windows opening on to a rose garden which was enhanced by a marble fountain forever in spray. The dining room was low and long, lighted by scores of candles and a gas chandelier. Most of the furniture was mahogany; dark and highly polished. The drawing rooms and study occupied the opposite side of the entrance hall, there being two drawing rooms, furnished beautifully with satin brocade upholstered chairs and settees, little tables crowded with precious ornaments, bowls of fresh flowers and pieces of silver. Brocade curtains dressed the windows and in one of the rooms stood a grand piano.

Most, if not all, South American families are many in number and this household had been a very large one too. Now, with the mother dead and sons and daughters married, this magnificent home was silenced, only being brought to life for a set time each day when the five noisy grandchildren from the neighbouring avenue visited their grandfather, and the entire place turned into bedlam immediately with laughter and shouts. The grandfather and a spinster daughter were the only occupants, and the children's mother was the only other daughter living within reasonable distance of the family home. There were, of course, many grown-up nieces and nephews, but they resided in other parts of the town. A huge family reunion would take place on special occasions and at Christmas.

The house needed a regiment of servants to maintain its splendour, for every room was kept alive with furniture, paintings and all the usual comforts. Nothing smelt musty or was allowed to harbour dust and neglect.

The children's ages ranged from twelve years to two. The first three were boys, and these were particularly my responsibility as I had to tutor them daily, giving each one individual periods of English lessons. Boys will be boys, and I had to grow accustomed to their roguish behaviour which often led me a dance. Their limited English would exasperate them when they were impatient to tell a joke, relate an incident or attempt a rag, for when they spoke to me they had strict instructions from their parents that they were to conduct all conversation in English in order to get full practical use of the language. They were all hot-tempered and quick to resort to quarrelling, but there were times, in comparison, when they were in affectionate moods, and when thus influenced each one would try to outdo the other to please me.

I knew the inside of their home pretty well at the end of the first month or so. It contained many rooms and, in fact, all of them occupied the ground floor. At the far end of the kitchen, however, a staircase led up to the cook's and maids' rooms which extended over the entire length of the kitchen and pantry.

I knew also, the immediate boundaries around the house and had played games with the children on the back lawn, but I had never explored the rambling spaces beyond a thick hedge which bordered the lawn and badminton court.

11

Patuqui

One day, with all the children away on an outing, I came to the house as usual, since I ate my meals there. With little to do I wandered through the grounds beyond that forbidding hedgerow. It was autumn, but the day was exceptionally warm. The sun beat down and not a leaf stirred.

As I strolled along, I was suddenly arrested by a loud barking – each bark was loud, long and drawn-out. Anxious to locate it, I moved on in the direction from whence it came. Imagine my surprise when, all this distance away from the house, I saw a large dog pulling on the end of a very short chain. The chain was secured tightly to a stake in the ground, and beside him was a small kennel. Around him, carelessly thrown, were hunks of raw meat, just a few inches short of his reach.

In the space of the first few minutes I grasped the whole scene. Here was an animal that would stand at least three feet high if he were able to get straight up on his legs, but this was impossible since his chain was too short to allow him to stand up at all. His body was so large that his small kennel only permitted his head and no more. Here were lumps of perfectly good meat, which would afford him a scrumptious meal, but thrown at tantalizing distance just out of his reach! There was no bowl of water, and no protection to which he could retire on a scorching summer's day or a cold winter's night. He looked ferocious, but how else could one expect a living creature to look when subjected to such thoughtless cruelties?

Despite his fierce appearance, he barked and wagged his sturdy tail, and attempted to jump up on seeing me, but the short chain restricted the poor animal's movements. Knowing nothing about him, however, and not sure of his reaction, I decided not to take a chance by going near to loosen his chain. Instead, I got hold of the lumps of meat and pushed them nearer so that he could enjoy them. Then, leaving him to his dinner, I ran speedily back to the house to make my investigations.

As I reached the kitchen door, I met the cook and quickly explained to her what I had seen. I must have sounded and looked extremely upset, but she did not seem one little bit perturbed. She gave me a toothy grin, adjusted her spectacles upon her shiny nose and replied, 'Why do you worry yourself, Señorita? It is only a dog.'

'Only a dog?' I questioned angrily. 'The poor animal is undergoing torture!'

I pushed past her and made straight for the drawing room where I found the children's mother. I asked if I might interrupt her, and she looked up from the book she was reading and invited me to take a seat. I told her about my discovery and when I concluded, she replied most serenely, 'Why, that must be Patuqui,' (pronounced Pa-thu-key). 'I'd never believe he's grown so big!'

'Haven't you seen him then?' I asked.

'Not recently. I last saw him when he was just over a year old.'

I looked at her in astonishment, trying to make sense of this conversation, and she continued, 'He was given as a gift to the boys a few years ago, but once he grew out of his puppy ways the children tired of him and the servants removed him to the outdoors.'

This left me almost dumbfounded, and she went on, 'He must be at least six years old. Did you say he's grown enormously?'

'Yes,' I replied, and begged her to accompany me to see him and the conditions under which he was existing.

'I can see that you care about animals,' she joked, and smiled as though the whole incident was amusing.

'It is no joking matter, madam,' I assured her.

Much to my surprise, she put down her book, stood up and said, 'Lead the way then, Miss Dorothy.'

We walked through the grounds, and she stopped now and again to admire a bush or some evergreen which she was seeing for the first time, since this part of the grounds was not familiar to her, even though it was the boundary of their own property. I pleaded with her not to depart from the immediate purport of our walk and she followed me.

Patuqui barked endlessly and pulled at his chain. She addressed him in Spanish, trying to silence him, but he took no notice and barked on. She explained that the servants were responsible for feeding him, but it seemed that the maid who brought him his meat once a day, having tired from the long walk through the grounds to this spot, could not be further bothered to place the meat in a plate beside him. Therefore, when she had come to a certain distance within his area, she carelessly flung the meat, not caring whether it had fallen within reach of the animal. If she hit the target, all was well and Patuqui got his meal that day. If she missed, he was left hungry, scratching and stretching in exasperation to try to reach that which he could not.

I felt thoroughly appalled over this state of affairs, but before I could plead his case, Madam turned to me and said, 'He needs a longer chain.'

'A longer chain?' I echoed.

She looked at me directly and explained, 'So that he can stand upright.'

'Oh, please, madam, why chain him at all? He's a lovely animal and should enjoy the freedom of these spacious grounds and the company of all of us.'

I took full advantage of the attention she was giving me and quickly pleaded for more of the comforts he should have, but when I concluded she was still not unduly concerned and started to walk away, saying, 'I'll tell Alfredo to get a longer chain in the morning.' Alfredo was one of her servants.

'We're not going to leave him in this fashion until then?' I almost shouted. The dog was not to suffer any longer than I could help, and I was determined to win my case so I persevered, 'Why can't I be allowed to go right away to the town centre and get him his chain now? It would take less than an hour if I catch a bus straightaway.'

'You do care for the animal, don't you?' she almost accused.

'Yes, I do,' I insisted. 'And I will not rest until relief is given. He has suffered enough.'

'There's an hour before lunch,' she said amicably. 'We'll drive down in the car now and get it.'

'You want to?' I queried with astonishment.

'Yes. You've melted my heart, as it were,' she confessed, with a charming smile.

'He needs a collar too,' I quickly added.

'A collar and chain. So shall it be,' she agreed good-humouredly.

Not content with my success so far, I requested, 'Why not take Patuqui with us?'

She turned her gaze on me, and then, with a pleasant smile, she replied, 'I can see that you are set to win!'

I quickly explained, 'If he were with us, we could measure him for the correct size.'

'All right,' she agreed. 'You fetch Patuqui and I'll get the car out.'

With what joy I bounded back to the animal in distress. I called his name as I approached him, and he wagged his tail and barked. Fearing nothing, and overjoyed with happiness for him, I loosened the chain, and he frolicked and almost galloped alongside me as I ran back to the house with him. He was an enormous animal, and not surprisingly he appeared unsteady on his legs. All the same, he kept up with me, barking and wagging his tail all the way. The cook and kitchen maids caught sight of me through the kitchen window and stared in astonishment, for they had never witnessed anything like this before. The lady of the house at the steering wheel – I flopped next to her, and this somewhat large uncontrollable animal squeezed into the spacious back seat! His paws were all over the white upholstery, and his head poked out curiously, first from this window and then that!

'Indeed, the Señorita from foreign country is completely mad!' I heard one of them remark.

Patuqui never stayed still whilst we sped on our way to find a pet shop in the town. He moved from side to side, peering out of the window one minute and poking a cold snout into the back of our necks, the next. He was wild with the excitement of his first ride in a car and, I daresay, of his first view of freedom from the uncomfortable imprisonment that had been his for so many years.

We finally reached the pet store, and he bounded in with us, sniffing at everything within his reach and knocking things down with his tremendous tail. We soon fitted him with a smart leather collar. It had steel studs on it and there was a silver disc upon which we were to have his name and address engraved. This suggestion came from the salesman and was graciously accepted. We bought him a long chain too, and while the situation was shaping out so successfully, I attempted a further request on his behalf.

'Have you seen the kennels on show?' I asked Madam. I knew I could get almost anything by now, for so novel had this shopping expedition proved to be to her that she was enjoying every minute of it.

'Yes, we'll buy another kennel,' she agreed, and with great difficulty the salesman measured Patuqui for size.

'He doesn't appear to have been trained to stand still,' he complained.

I just smiled. Little did this pleasant young man, having twice been knocked over by Patuqui, realize that the poor animal was baffled by his newly acquired freedom.

As the kennel was too large to bring back with us, orders were placed for its delivery to be made to the house later that afternoon. On the drive back, Patuqui still remained excited, and he looked fine in his new collar. After a while, I plucked up enough courage to venture, 'May I have Patuqui, please? He'll be wonderful company for me at the cottage and he can act as a watchdog at night. I do get pretty lonesome sometimes.'

'I don't see any reason why you shouldn't be allowed to have him, Miss Dorothy,' Madam consented, and this made my day, for I was so happy with the prospect of keeping him beside me.

At the end of that day, I ceremoniously walked him down the avenue to my cottage. Word had got around to both the houses, by now, of the day's happenings which were the most unusual of events that had ever taken place in this grand and dignified household.

Patuqui took to me as a fish would to water. He lacked any training, but with love and perseverance I had him sit, lie, stop and heel in next to no time, and he became my faithful and obedient friend over the months that followed. Each day I walked him to the children's house, and whilst I conducted my lessons he remained obediently stretched out under my table or upon the hearthrug.

The children were bewitched and bewildered by him. The two older boys remembered him vaguely, but the three younger children did not know Patuqui at all and had been completely unaware of his existence.

Somehow, none of the children showed great fondness for him. Whether his great size had something to do with their indifference, I did not know. They had obviously not been trained and encouraged to love animals, but I knew that, given time, I would remedy this, and accordingly I set about finding a way to begin.

It was part of the routine that the children went to the park every evening between four and five o'clock, and I struck on the idea that if I volunteered to chaperone them it would afford an excellent opportunity for them to get to know Patuqui at leisure and at the same time allow the dog the exercise he so needed. So I had a word with the children's nanny who usually took them on this outing, and she agreed to my proposal.

The park, or El Prado as it was called, was about ten minutes' walk from our avenue. Once we reached the park grounds Patuqui was taken off his chain and would scamper about happily. He would chase the boys on their cycles and bound back to the girls and me. The three boys usually cycled to the park whilst the two little girls walked with Patuqui and me. Instantly the boys commenced a ball game, Patuqui would dash forward and confiscate the ball! His action would raise loud laughter from the children, and by this frolic he won their love and admiration. Often when the little girls complained of being tired, I showed them how strong and kind Patuqui was in offering them a ride on his back! By the end of a week, a distinct change of attitude was apparent and Patuqui was accepted as their playmate.

Great Danes, although very large animals, are gentle creatures and love children. They make excellent companions for the young, and I wanted the children to know and understand all about this pet which was gradually becoming part of the family circle, so with gentle persuasion I got them interested in everything about him. I suggested they try to draw a picture of Patuqui and get the harlequin colouring correct. I gave them each a long piece of string to measure his length from nose to tip of tail. I allowed them to practise their own commands on him, and all the while he thoroughly enjoyed every bit of the attention he was receiving.

From then on, the children became so absorbed in Patuqui that they were observing for themselves his various moods and mannerisms and drawing my attention to them. I felt now that he had established a place in their hearts and I had no more fears for his happiness. How wrong I was!

Dorothy and Patuqui, 1952

12

Part 1 ~ The Estancia

Most weekends the family went to the *estancia* where they had their cattle ranch and country house. These outings always caused a great rumpus and proved exciting and enjoyable. The children's nanny and I joined the family on these occasions and, split up in two parties, we would set off in two limousines early on Saturday mornings, returning late on Sunday nights.

The ranch stretched over many acres of land and there must have been quite a few hundred head of cattle. A large number of gauchos were employed on the ranch and life within these environments galloped past fast and furiously. Gauchos are the world's roughest riders and I had the thrill of witnessing their skills on horseback. This was not only at a normal day's rounding up of the cattle but especially during *Semana Santa*, or Holy Week in the English language, when the breaking-in of the horses takes place each year and gauchos from all over the country assemble at special arenas to display their skills and compete for coveted prizes.

The minute we arrived at the *estancia*, the boys would waste no time in making a quick change, donning Gaucho outfits and sombreros and heading for the stables where their own personal horses would be. They were expert riders, as most Uruguayan children of the wealthy families were. They went to no special riding schools to learn the art, for the *estancia*, being second home to them, they develop the characteristics of its life naturally. From babyhood they mount a pony as expertly as a kiddie would climb a chair, and as they grow older the change from pony to horse comes automatically and without fear. Understanding their horses, too, came as second nature, I discovered.

Though I had to teach the children many things about Patuqui, I found that their knowledge of the horse was wider than mine. The girls were still too young for anything bigger than ponies and each had her own pony to ride. Unafraid and fully accustomed to speed upon four legs, the children would mount their animals and become part of the immediate setting. But I, not being a horsewoman, kept my feet firmly on the ground, even though the family presented me with a beautiful white horse for my use and many of the gauchos offered to give me riding lessons.

Nanny might have been a rider in her younger days no doubt, and she had been with the family for well over fifteen years. Her love for this sport brought a sparkle to her eyes when she talked of it but, heavy from middle age now, she kept away from the horses.

The country mansion squatted imposingly upon a brilliant green carpet of soft grass. It had no garden surrounding it, but fields of open space sloped in all directions, interrupted on one side by an enormous open air swimming pool. It had exquisite shades of blue and green mosaic tiles embedded within its structure and these gave the water a vivid hue. There were two diving boards and one side of the pool was lined with changing rooms.

A large staff of servants was maintained permanently at the mansion and even the children's wardrobes were fully equipped with clothes, thus eliminating the tiresome task of taking week-end cases or bringing back a load of soiled clothing.

Throughout the day we kept to the open, spending a few hours in the luxury of the pool. Lunch was served in the open under the shade of trees and consisted mainly of enormous steaks, cooked very rare. The South American, I learnt, only enjoyed his steak if it bled profusely on the plate! In comparison, I preferred my steak well done and this completely amazed the cook.

In the evening we reposed in comfortable chairs under a starry sky and listened to the music and songs of the gauchos as they played on their guitars. For a special treat, the gauchos and their womenfolk would sometimes entertain us with spectacular Latin folk dances.

Part 2 ~ Carnival

One of the memorable occasions I witnessed in South America was Carnival Week. It is a time of great rejoicing when the whole country stops work and is hit by a holiday spirit. The roads and streets are festooned with coloured bunting and massed bands and small groups of musicians tramp the streets, their lively rhythm booming loudly during all hours of the day and night. Doors never close and lights never dim. Children and grown-ups, rich and poor alike, become caught up in the contagion of the street frivolities, and colourful floats bearing the local bevy, each member a beauty queen in her own right, plough through the dancing crowds along the roads. It is a time for romance, fun and music, and I was soon captured by the merriment and delightful madness.

At times of jollification, however, whether it be in a private dwelling or a state into which the entire nation has entered, some household pets suffer as a result of their owners' carelessness or thoughtlessness while they celebrate, and at carnival time many pets are intimidated by the noise of fireworks exploding around and above them. When loose, they may be seen running frantically in search of a place of refuge, becoming tangled up with the legs of the hundreds of wildly excited dancers and spectators along the roads. Those dogs that happened to be secured in the grounds of their dwelling houses suffered even more from the additional handicap of not being able to flee for protection as each new bunch of fireworks and crackers burst around them.

During the entire week, I kept Patuqui comforted in the cottage. I never left him alone, asking a girlfriend to take charge in the hours when I was obliged to leave my cottage. Even in my company, he whimpered and trembled each time an explosion echoed in the distance, and I wished there was some way in which I could have comforted the less fortunate pets in the neighbourhood.

Los Gauchos, Montevideo 1952

13

Mistrust

After the strains of carnival had died away, life returned to a more sober pattern and I once again settled down to my lessons with the children. In the large house next door lived a family with ten children, and among the younger ones was a set of male twins. They were aged eight and, being companionable to the two younger boys of our household, they were frequent visitors. Although always accompanied by their governess, they proved to be a handful and were boisterous and naughty. No amount of correction disciplined them and, apart from their rascality, they were positively cruel. I had to keep a close eye on Patuqui all the time that the twins were around lest they plagued him with this torture or that. One of them carried a pistol in his belt and so keenly disposed was he to injuring or taking life that he would even aim a crack shot at the clock in the study, whenever our friendly cuckoo announced the hour!

Between two and four o'clock each day the household servants, having cleared away the luncheon things and put the kitchen in order, would retire to their rooms upstairs for their siesta. One afternoon, hearing a lot of excited hilarity coming from the kitchen, I went to investigate this uproar and saw the twins, together with my charges, grouped around the cooker. All four pairs of grubby hands were holding down the lid of a large saucepan.

'What have you got there?' I demanded.

The merriment died immediately as four pairs of eyes turned on me, portraying guilt.

'A frog,' one little voice faltered.

I raced forward, switched off the cooker, uncovered the saucepan and espied, to my great horror, a large helpless frog squatting in some shallow water.

I seemed to have intercepted this cruelty in the nick of time, for their object was to boil the poor creature alive! They started off their experiment with cold water that had not quite become lukewarm. Quickly replacing the lid, I ordered the young vandals to fall into line and led them to the bottom of the garden to the fish pond, from whence they had captured the frog, and bade them stand still and watch whilst I returned it to the safety of its home.

Relating the incident later on to the cook brought little compassion for the unfortunate creature, for she seemed more concerned about the cooking utensil being tainted than the agonies that could have been inflicted on the helpless creature had the boys been successful in their evildoing.

Alas, there is no easy way to suppress the desire to be cruel, in a child, unless the child in question is one's very own when appropriate punishment can be administered to fit the crime. When handling other people's offspring one is obliged to tone down one's voice, to stay one's hand from landing the well-deserved slap on a spot where it would hurt and resort instead to the less effective method of telling the child that he is doing wrong. Words do not always carry weight unless the parents give support to them, and if they themselves lack a sense of compassion, then nothing can be achieved and in this particular instance I found myself surrounded by non-supporters. However, I persevered and tried to convert the grown-ups around me in the hope that, by example, the children would alter their villainous tendencies. When my charges were alone with me I could get them to conform without great difficulty and I had made such big strides with them in our association with Patuqui that I almost complimented myself on success in this field. Too soon came the horrible moment of disillusion!

It was well over six months by now since my first meeting with Patuqui and all that ensued, and, it being my afternoon off, I proposed spending some of it in the town. The children, on hearing that I was going out, asked if they could have Patuqui to play with, and on my consenting the boys came to my cottage and collected him. I had no fears for the dog and the children promised to return him to the cottage by eight o'clock that night, the time that I expected to be back from the town.

I met my two girlfriends at our usual rendezvous restaurant for tea. We then visited the shops and at seven o'clock I bade them goodbye and boarded the streetcar that would take me home. Later that same evening, I was to attend a dinner dance and my escort was expected just before nine. It was close on eight o'clock when I returned to my cottage. I had almost an hour to get dressed for my date, and whilst I prepared myself I listened out for the children's footsteps, anticipating Patuqui's safe return.

Half an hour ticked by, but there was no sign of their coming, so I decided to slip into something quickly, hurry to the main house and telephone the children. As I made these mental notes, however, I suddenly heard a scratching at my cottage door. I could not imagine that the children had allowed Patuqui to return across the avenue alone, and hurried to let him in. Imagine my horror when I discovered him standing at the threshold with a tortured look in his eyes and his tail sticking straight out behind him, encased and heavy with thick tar! It was covered completely and thoroughly from base to its tip. He whimpered, but made no further movement towards me. He looked terrified and his legs and body trembled. Who had done it? How? Why? These questions raced through my mind as I reassured him gently and examined his tail closely with my eyes.

I searched my mind frantically for as to how to act in order not to give the dog any further discomfort. Who could I call?

The servants in the grandfather's house would not be interested in my requests for help. I remembered, too, that there was a big cocktail party in progress. This was to be followed by a dinner and, therefore, they would be too busy to attend to such trivialities as an animal with a sticky tail! The story would probably prove amusing and raise a laugh instead of a sigh of compassion.

With the realisation of my helplessness I paced my cottage impatiently. Suddenly, the bright headlamps of a car lit up my window and front door and an engine purred to a stop. I saw my escort for the evening step out in his immaculate white dinner jacket and stride up the short path to my cottage. Greeting him with my distress, I pointed to Patuqui who still stood motionless in a tormented silence.

'Have you got a knife?' Roberto asked.

'No,' I replied, 'but I'll soon fetch one from the main house.'

I dashed out across the grounds and on hurrying back, I found that Roberto had stripped off his dinner jacket and his shirt sleeves were rolled up ready to tackle the all important duty. We placed sheets of newspaper over the carpet of my sitting room, then, very patiently and with a steady hand, he began the tiresome procedure of scraping off the layers of tar. This must have taken the best part of an hour. Patuqui stood obediently all through this ordeal, and his tail now suddenly drooped.

Roberto then drew out some petrol from the tank of his car and swiftly, but gently, he soaked off the remains of the dark viscous mixture that had embedded itself in the hair. Whilst he did this he instructed me to get ready some warm soapy water in the bath.

We led Patuqui to the bathroom and between us we lifted him up and into the water. While Roberto held on to him firmly,

I shampooed his tail gently, and at last it was back to normal! At least, it looked perfectly clean and normal from the outside, but whether it hurt, itched or stung, I would not know. Patuqui appeared relieved and seemed happy as he lay stretched out on the carpet, slowly wagging it when we addressed him. As for our dinner dance date, it had automatically been hit on the head, for as Roberto unrolled his shirt sleeves and made ready to leave, the cathedral clock banged out the midnight hour. Three solid hours had we toiled over an unfortunate animal's tail. The orchid that Roberto had brought for me still lay in its glamorous satin-lined presentation box, and the lovely expensive chiffon dress I had so carefully chosen for this evening's date remained unused.

As I bade Roberto goodnight I noticed that his smart black evening trousers and highly polished shoes were spattered from the soapy water that Patuqui had splashed him with.

In the morning I let it be known throughout the households about Patuqui's ordeal of the previous night, but no culprit came forward to confess. When I questioned them, the children sniggered and thought the whole episode funny. As for the servants, they merely shrugged their shoulders and appeared disinterested. Later that afternoon, however, quite unexpectedly I discovered to my regret, that it was the twins and two of our boys who had indulged in this vile deed.

Our chauffeur came across four small shirts disposed of in one of the garages and, knowing them to be the children's, he was conveying them back to the house when I encountered him. The big telltale smudges of thick black tar on them revealed the whole painful truth, and I never entrusted Patuqui to the children again.

14

A Royal Event

Queen Elizabeth II of England was to be crowned the following year, and the prospect of witnessing a Coronation, an event so rare, could not be missed, so that it attracted all those who could afford it, to make a beeline for Britain. I was very tempted and, much as I had grown to love South America and regretted the thought of leaving the wonderful friends I had gathered about me, I, too, decided to wend my way to London for this great occasion.

Without hesitation, I drew on the bulk of my savings, raced to the shipping offices of the Royal Mail Lines and booked myself a passage on the *Alcantara*, bound for Southampton. Having done so, I then broke the news to my employers and my friends. Everyone received my announcement with sadness, and it was then that I realized the amount of affection and regard that they all had for me. The children set up a hue and cry, imploring me not to leave and asking whether, after the Coronation, I would return to them. My personal friends got together and organized a big farewell party for me in one of their apartments. It was one of the finest parties I had attended in a long time, but hearts lay heavy behind the smiles and laughter. My party coincided with the usual New Year's Eve celebrations and this made it a doubly nostalgic gathering. I was to sail from Montevideo on the third day of January.

A few weeks before I was due to leave, thoughts of Patuqui's welfare distracted me. I felt crushed with sadness about bidding him farewell and unashamedly confessed this to my employer. I told her that no matter where my journeys took me, I would be reminded of him and I feared he might fret for me.

We had often taken Patuqui to the *estancia*, and I remembered how he enjoyed the open spaces and the great fuss that the gauchos made over him. They seemed to care genuinely for their animals and I decided that it would be more appropriate for Patuqui to be transferred permanently to the *estancia* instead of being subjected to the lonely existence that would be his once I had left the scene. Undoubtedly, he would have been placed in the care of the household servants again and committed to a chain and kennel, and I could not bear the thought of his falling victim to this cruel life sentence.

It was agreed that my suggestion be carried out and on the last weekend before I was due to sail we made a journey to the *estancia*. It was a sad and memorable occasion. Indeed, it was a heartbreaking one for me. We spent a splendid weekend, of course, but when we prepared to leave for home on Sunday evening, Patuqui remained behind. He seemed to search me for an explanation when we all piled into the cars, leaving him in the midst of the gauchos. I kept my head turned, gazing at him through the rear window as we drove away, and felt a slight easing when one of the gauchos bent close to him and appeared to be kissing his head!

Dorothy with the pigeons in Trafalgar Square, 1953

15

Part 1 ~ Bound for England

I had never been to England before and was excited about the trip. I had heard a lot about the country and I was now looking forward to seeing it. I informed my brother and his wife of my intended arrival and they extended a warm welcome to their home, in the picturesque village of Baston, as a landing base before I journeyed down to London to set up home temporarily.

During the length of my travels and through all my experiences, the tug to return home to India came in regular spasms, therefore it was inevitable that I would one day be homeward bound. This was a worthwhile opportunity to use England as the halfway mark on the sentimental journey back to the Orient.

The voyage to Britain took eighteen days. I was given a grand send-off when I embarked, for all my friends came to the port. Numerous bouquets had been delivered in their names to my cabin, but I saw these only after the ship had sailed when I went below, having waved goodbye to the colourful group until they were specks no more! What a delightful surprise it was to enter what looked like a miniature florists! I read the cards carefully and cut them off, placing them in a neat pile ready for me to acknowledge by the time we reached Santos which was the first port of call.

I remembered my encounter with the regiments of crabs at this particular place, so I decided against going ashore and handed a large packet of letters to another passenger to post. Then came Rio. I went ashore with friends I had newly acquired on board, and memories of my first impressions of this beautiful seaport came flooding back. Again, it was summer and the Copacabana beach was alive with tanned bodies and a blaze of colour. The next two ports of call were Babina and Pernambuco which were both delightful places to visit. From then on, we headed for Las Palmas where we docked for a day. A party of us filled a taxi and went on a sightseeing tour. We drove to the heights of the Grand Canary, where canaries abide in millions, turning the sky yellow with their throng.

Canaries cost next to nothing to buy in these islands and almost every passenger ashore acquired a bird to take back on board. The sad part about this, however, is that they were not permitted to take the birds into England, and on arriving at Lisbon instructions came from the Captain for all canaries to be taken off board, and little boys and girls whose parents had foolishly and thoughtlessly satisfied their children's whims for these pets found to their disgust, horror or sadness that the birds had to be freed.

Lisbon was a spectacular harbour with some very attractive buildings. Among these was a superior restaurant with a dance hall. There were many interesting shops too, and a party of us left to explore the sights of this fine town, deciding to return for the dinner and dance at the port before embarking at midnight.

From Lisbon we sailed onwards to the picturesque port of Vigo. Once again my fellow passengers and I made a general assault on the shopping area and armed ourselves with a quantity of the local souvenirs, to return with lovely memories of the day spent ashore.

From Vigo onwards, the weather changed dramatically and especially as we neared Cherbourg. Changing into heavy winter wear, we went ashore to practise our French and make the most of our outing at this last port of call before we disembarked at Southampton the following day.

Typical of the British weather, which I had previously been warned about, a few hours after sailing from Cherbourg the *Alcantara* was enveloped in a blanket of fog. This hazard at sea proved to be very frightening and passengers were instructed to keep to their cabins or to the lounges and not to venture on deck. The ship anchored for a certain length of time and there was much anxiety among the passengers as to our safe arrival.

Much to our relief, however, the fog lifted almost as suddenly as it had descended upon us, and once again we were happily speeding on our way. We approached Southampton at about three o'clock in the afternoon in a ray of watery sunlight. The atmosphere bit into our fingertips and tingled our toes!

Journey's end always brings mixed feelings. On the one hand there is the tremendous joy of being reunited with loved ones and on the other hand the pain, however slight, of bidding farewell to fellow passengers who, having shared with you in the various experiences, happy or otherwise, over several weeks of being thrown together, were now necessarily making an exit from your life, each to depart in his or her completely different direction, our paths perhaps never to meet again. These thoughts of pending farewell brought a deep sense of nostalgia to me as the time drew near to part company with the marvellous happy friendships that had been established.

Part 2 ~ First Impressions

On the quayside stretched a long line of heavily clad people in sombre colour. They stood almost motionless, afraid to give vent to their feelings, except for the odd hand or two which ventured to wave a greeting in defiance of the reservation that otherwise prevailed. Certainly there was no demonstration of the wild excitement, shouts and cheers and hilarious handclapping I had grown accustomed to witnessing at all the ports of call on my previous voyages. This quiet, controlled behaviour was absolutely frightening in comparison, and had I been the stranger that I was, arriving in this strange new land with no kin to meet me, I would have been positively scared to put my foot ashore, so cold did the reception appear. The *Alcantara*, meanwhile, had glided into her berth, and I was glad to know that my relatives were standing, also reservedly, somewhere in that silent line, waiting to greet and welcome me warmly, nevertheless, once I was within close proximity.

This first impression of the British public altered, however, as I journeyed through the country later. I found that these reserved exteriors were not as forbidding as they appeared to be, but that the nation as a whole was just as warm-hearted, friendly and talkative as any of my amorous and over-demonstrative Latin American friends.

After the tall skyscrapers, massive houses, enormous ranches and immense open spaces I had been accustomed to in Uruguay, my first notion of England, as British Railways sped me through the Midlands, was of how diminutive the houses and fields were. I felt as Gulliver must have done in Lilliput. The largest house gave the impression of a cottage and the first cottages I saw in the village of Baston resembled outsized dolls' houses, but this undoubtedly represented the cosy, homely way of British life.

Part 3 ~ An Awakening

I enjoyed a few weeks in Baston, but knew it was time to make for London if I were to succeed in obtaining digs before it became difficult or impossible, due to the influx of tourists. Therefore, bidding my relatives farewell, I started out for London.

The sights that the capital offered were familiar to me having seen them in picture books, history books, postcards and British Movietone newsreels that used to reach us in far-off India. A sudden thrill hit me, all the same, when I realized that this was no scene I was admiring on the screen but that I was actually standing in Trafalgar Square, surrounded by friendly pigeons and looking up at Nelson's Column! I strolled up the Mall and eventually came face to face with Buckingham Palace. I gazed with awe at the lofty guardsman rooted like a statue and, plucking up courage, I handed my camera to a bystander, strode smartly up to the handsome soldier, fell in beside him and heard the click from my cameraman! This picture I was assured would cause much envy and interest to my friends at home.

Leaving the area of the Palace, I wended my way towards a bus stop and boarded a bus that would take me to the Royal Park, generally called Hyde Park, in which rests the large lake called the Serpentine. As I peered excitedly out of the window at the passing scenery, the ever flowing traffic and the hurrying pedestrians, all culminating to create the tempo of busy capitals the world over, our bright red double-decker pulled up abruptly, and some of us slid on our seats from the unexpected halt. Immediately behind and alongside us, all the traffic had pulled to a stop and we wondered what had caused this hold-up. Drivers of the various vehicles within the vicinity of our bus appeared patient and good-humoured despite the unscheduled delay, and the word quickly got around in the bus, from the passengers who had a front seat view, that a mother duck, followed by a brood of ducklings, had decided to cross the road at this juncture. There they went, waddling happily across from one side of the road to the other, while a part of London's traffic stood still!

What joy this sight evoked as I quickly transferred the scene in my mind, placing it on a busy street in the Orient, where little consideration would have been shown and where, in comparison, one driver would have competed with the other to eliminate the little creatures under their wheels. This humane and civilised thought for God's helpless creatures impressed me to a point that left me in no doubt at all that here was a country to which all furred and feathered creatures should have been destined. This incident was my introduction to the animal world in England.

I learnt, as days multiplied into weeks and weeks into months, more and more about the societies and the Acts of Parliament that sought to protect dumb creatures from man's cruel hands. It was absolute bliss to walk out on the roads and not see them littered with strays. There are special Dogs' Homes for such unfortunates, where care and love is given until a suitable owner can be found. It was apparent to me that persons who kept pets had them for the joy and companionship they offered and loved them for what they were. The law took action, I noted from some isolated cases of cruelty reported in the newspapers, against any owner ill-treating his animal. Cats were goddesses in the homes where they lived and dogs ruled mistresses sometimes!

What a lovely idea it would be if, just for a day all over the world, the positions were reversed and the rider became the weary horse, the glutton was confined to a kennel and dry bone, the naughty schoolboy turned into a thrush guarding her eggs! If the tables were transposed I believe that only good would come out of the experience and man would become dog's best friend.

Part 4 ~ Mr Chips and Master Toots

I was comfortably settled in furnished rooms with a most kind and generous landlady. She owned a prosperous business, the shop being situated beneath the spacious flat which also belonged to her. The only other occupants in our flat were a young English spaniel called Mr Chips and a dear young kitten called Master Toots. Mr Chips had a black and white roan coat and Master Toots had sleek black fur that felt as soft as velvet. Beneath his chin was a small white spot which looked like a stud or button.

Mr Chips had his own comfortable armchair in the sitting room and this was kept clean and in spotless condition for him alone. If a guest unknowingly made for that particular seat, which matched three others in the room, they being a complete set, the hostess had no hesitation in

Master Toots

politely explaining that it was booked for Mr Chips. It stood near the large window where the sunshine caught it, and it overlooked the busy main road, and all day, while his mistress ran her business premises, he would sit curled up in the depths of comfort and watch the world go by! Mr Chips was so pampered with consideration and kindness that there were times when he himself must have doubted whether he was a dog or a person! This upbringing made him particularly helpless on occasions, for he never proved to be a watchdog. On the contrary, he was terrified of callers and when the doorbell sounded he would cower and whimper, making for the safety of the bedroom. We then had to pick him up and console him! There were also problems created when my landlady, keen on the cinema and theatre, sought a night out. Prior to my joining the household, she was obliged to hire a baby-sitter for Mr Chips as he was too timid to be left alone, but on my taking up residence with her, and having established that I was an animal lover, she entrusted me with him. We made it a routine from then on that I would sit with Mr Chips on the nights when she wished to have her entertainment.

Mr Chips liked being taken for his walks to the nearby park, and each evening we took it in turns to exercise him. We always used the back entrance, therefore Mr Chips was only acquainted with that side of the building and, apart from having a romp with Master Toots on the back lawn, he had never seen the front of the shop. This opened out from the shop door on to the pavement and adjoining shops.

For the duration of my stay in England I occupied myself with a situation in a local office, so each lunch hour I returned to the flat and enjoyed a meal with my landlady. One afternoon on my arrival, I found her very distressed, and in tears she explained that Mr Chips had gone missing. She believed that one of the tradesmen had carelessly left the gate open and the dog must have wandered out. She had searched all round the back for him with no success, and he had now been gone for two hours. I too, became extremely anxious for his safety and, forgoing lunch, I set out to make my search. After a half an hour I had to abandon it, however, as it was almost time to return to the office. But just as I was about to leave and she prepared to send out an SOS to the local newspaper, offering a handsome reward for his return, the telephone rang, and imagine our delight to be told by the shopkeeper three doors away that the dog was there! Apparently he had been stationed in the same position outside their shop for the past two hours. They had noticed him earlier, but, believing that the owner had positioned him there to await his return, the shopkeeper took no action. Now, having realized the length of time that the dog had been there, whining softly by this time, one of the shop assistants made bold to search his collar for an address, fully convinced that the owner had forgotten his pet. On investigation, he found the disc which gave his name and the telephone number where his owner could be contacted.

Needless to say, we both exclaimed with happy relief at finding him safe and sound, though he seemed a trifle bewildered by his unusual experience. This incident was a proof of how Mr Chips lacked the ability to find his way back home, which doubtless would have come almost naturally to any other dog. However, he had learnt his lesson and never again wandered from the back garden, even when the gate was left unlocked.

Master Toots was very fond of Mr Chips and followed him closely about the rooms. When Mr Chips settled on the carpet or in his favourite chair, Master Toots was quick to join him. He seemed to find pleasure in cuddling up close to the dog, and many a time we found him earnestly licking and grooming Mr Chips's long curly-haired ears, which seemed to please the dog immensely. At playtime Mr Chips was inclined to forget himself and as he and the kitten chased a ball around, he would suddenly divert his attention and knock poor Master Toots about instead of the ball! He would grasp him in his jaws and shake him vigorously from side to side, but the kitten never seemed to take fright or to retaliate. There is so much joy and amusement to be derived from household pets and we had many a hearty laugh over these frolics.

Mr Chips sometimes portrayed the reactions of a spoiled child, prone to complain to its mother of some seeming ill-treatment or reprimand it had received from another grown-up, and if ever I checked him for teasing Master Toots unnecessarily he would immediately run to his mistress and, by his attitude, she would know that I had spoken harshly to him. So obviously did he sulk that I would be obliged to apologise to him! With such a human dog around, I found that I had to watch my p's and q's. It is not that I disliked Mr Chips. He was gentle and lovable and I adored him, but I did not fully condone his attitude towards Master Toots, though the kitten appeared quite capable of handling the situation.

Part 5 ~ Coronation Day

Fully taken up with my work, the pets at home and week-end sightseeing tours, I had not noticed how the months had slipped by. It was now the month of June, and on the second it would be Coronation Day. I prepared, as the thousands of others did, to make tracks on the night previous to a vantage point along the route on which the procession would pass.

One expected warmth and brilliant sunshine at this time of year but, unfortunately, the weather proved most disappointing. It brought a drizzle which kept on throughout the night and the temperature dropped quite considerably. It was an unusual experience for me as I had never before spent the night in the open. However, I soon became acquainted with the crowds milling around me, and they seemed a jovial lot. The hours were passed singing the popular community songs and some vendors cashed in on sales of tea, coffee and hot dogs.

In the course of the night the crowds had so thickened that I took another spectator's advice and transferred my stand from Hyde Park Corner to Oxford Street where, I was assured, I would get a better and closer view, it being less crowded there. The only disadvantage was that I would not see the procession until its return journey from the Abbey, which meant many extra hours of patient waiting.

But at long last the great moment arrived, and amid cheers and applause the procession wended its way past me. The first sight of the coach with its beautiful royal occupant took my breath away. What glamour! What pomp! The long hours of waiting in the cold and damp had been worth it.

Dorothy with a Grenadier Guard
outside Buckingham Palace

16

Assurance

Soon after this tremendous event I began to prepare for my journey back to India, and I booked a passage on the *Chusan* which was due to sail late in December. As I progressed with my travel arrangements, my landlady suddenly decided to sell her business and take over another in a new area. So, with the premises up for quick sale, I sought alternative living accommodation. We parted regretfully and my connections with Master Toots and Mr Chips ended. Soon after I moved, the sale was concluded and my landlady and her pets started for their new address which was a long distance from mine.

The voyage back to India was exciting. I was impatient to return, to meet my relatives and friends again and to tell them about my interesting travels. The past twelve months in England had temporarily dimmed my memory of the existence of suffering animals in other parts of the world. Not witnessing any form of cruelty or indifference to dumb creatures in my immediate surroundings, I became accustomed to no longer looking for the stray or to being tormented with pity for them. I had no cause for anxiety about their well-being and happiness.

Then, all at once I was jolted out of my composure, for as I set foot ashore at Bombay, I saw a half-starved mongrel cringe as someone aimed a brick at him ... I knew then that I had returned to take up the threads which I had left off three long years ago! Nothing had changed in my absence. Nothing ever would ...

This story has no end. The telling of a love story such as this concludes only when the narrator's life ends. Even after that, for years to come, the world will still be orbiting in God's keeping. Man and beast will continue to share it, and the human being endowed with the extra-special sense of compassion will forever identify himself or herself on behalf of our dumb friends.